I0413188

Table of Contents

60 day FREE membership to the Survivalist Prepper Academy.

Access to more online resources with downloads and free stuff.

Access the "Intro to Prepping Course"

All free with when you purchase "Be Prepared for anyything"

Find out how to access all of this free content at the end of this book.

A Little About Lisa & I at SurvivalistPrepper.net

As history has shown us over and over again that we as people, civilizations or as an entire planet are not invincible. Could I be wasting my time and money preparing? Maybe. Could everything collapse tomorrow destroying life as we know it? Could be. But I will be ready to defend myself from everyone caught off guard and unprepared for survival and trying to take advantage of my survival preparations.

We want to educate everyone about some of the very real scenarios that are possible in the world we live in today. Everyone knows that an earthquake can cause millions in damage and loss of life but how many people are really paying attention to what is going on right outside their front door? The government has made us (some of us) so reliant on them that we forget that we have the power, but we are losing that power every day because we are content and don't want to fix something that isn't broke. Well I'm here to tell you IT'S BROKE! And if we don't fix it soon we could end up just like the citizens of North Korea, Not allowed to express ourselves, not allowed to protect ourselves and complete slaves to this country.

Why did we start the SurvivalistPrepper.net website?

We are not the overboard tinfoil hat wearing conspiracy theorists, we are just like you, everyday Americans that enjoy the freedoms that this country offers. But over the last 10 years it has become increasingly clear that something really bad is going to happen that changes our lives forever. Maybe it's because as we get older and more responsible and the protection of me and my family takes precedence over everything else.

I have a couple of other websites (for business) but our website SurvivalistPrepper.net has nothing to do with that, our website and this book were created because we are passionate about being prepared. Our website is about staying up to date on current events and learning the skills to survive and protect your loved ones.

I created SurvivalistPrepper.net because I am always looking around the internet at other prepper and survival websites it just seemed logical to start my own. Not only because I have been prepping and learning survival skills for a while now, but because I want to help spread the word and educate people about how to acquire the skill set that gives them the best chance for survival no matter what the future brings.

What Is Our Philosophy On Survival And Prepping?

You might hear people talking about how you need to be in the middle of nowhere with $100,000 worth of guns and ammunition and a highly fortified perimeter around your property but this is just not possible for the average person on a budget. Our philosophy on being prepared is being educated about what you will need to do considering the environment you live in. The process of bugging out will be completely different for a family who lives in an urban area as opposed to someone who already lives in a rural area.

If the SHTF and you live in a highly populated area the odds are you will need to act fast, you will have 200,000 people right next door that all want your stuff. If you live in a rural area you better get ready because everyone from the urban area might be headed your way. When the SHTF there could be a mass exodus from the city because everyone will try to get as far away from the madness as possible.

Both situations require a different type of prepping and a completely different survival strategy, if you live in the city are you going to try and defend your family while everyone else flees? Are you going to try to get out of dodge with the 200,000 others? Whatever you decide you need to have a plan...a well thought out plan!

If you live in a rural area how do you plan on protecting your family when the scared masses from the city come to you expecting your help? How will you protect your family and property?

A good survival plan does not depend on how many guns you have or how big your food supply is. A good survival plan all depends on how well prepared you are to defend those things you have and keep the supplies you depend on for survival. Most of us cannot spend every extra dollar we have on expensive guns, ammo, MRE's or underground bunkers. But we can learn how to survive when all of that is taken away from us.

Our goal here is to build a community of likeminded people and learn from each other and teach each other. Please join our mailing list for the latest information about current events we feel could have life changing impact on us as United States citizen, as well as our thoughts about what we can do about it. We gladly extend an invitation to anyone who feels the same way about surviving any economic collapse, natural disaster or any unforeseen event that could turn our world upside down.

Be Ready For It All – An Intro to Prepping

About The Book

Why do we need another book about prepping? Quite honestly prepping isn't brain surgery, and quite honestly there are some great book out there about prepping and surviving any sort of disaster. But for every good book that is out there, there are 10 books written to scare you into buying them or just don't have the information you want and need.

These books that are out there just to get your money do you no good. These books are written to get you when you are most vulnerable. When we are just beginning to open your eyes to prepping it is usually because we have had a personal doomsday situation happen to us or because we just can't ignore the problems we face as a country or entire planet these days. And that is how they get you, they promise to give you all the keys to insure your survival, but the truth is, these books only give you the basics and what any seasoned pepper already knows.

When you start prepping and preparing for your future you need to know where to start, and I don't mean how much food and water you need to store. You need to know the why? And you need to know the how? It does you no good to have a month's worth of food stockpiled if it is built on debt and you can't pay your rent.

You've taken the biggest step so far by deciding to take your life into your own hands and not rely on government or outside sources for your survival.

As a matter of fact the definition of a prepper is just that "An individual or group that prepares or makes preparations in advance of, or prior to, any change in normal circumstances, without substantial resources from outside sources"

When you first become interested in prepping and you start to realize that everything is not all sunshine and roses, nothing is guaranteed, and nothing is as wonderful as they would like us to believe. You begin to realize that our comfortable little society is not very stable at all and because all society's fall, it's only a matter of time before we do to.

With all the advances we have made in medicine and technology we have become complaisant and dependent on it. And most people don't fully understand how brittle our society really is. Now don't get me wrong, I am not saying that everything is going to crumble in the next few months, or our county is on the brink of collapse, but I'm not willing to say that a SHTF scenario isn't a very real possibility either.

When we hop into our car and head to work we have no doubt that we will make it there, but as we know unexpected problems arise all the time. This could be something simple like a flat tire to an accident that leaves you injured or possible worse.

The same thing goes for larger scale events, we get complaisant because not much changes from day to day, we can go years without something terrible happening to us and then one day when we least expect it something like 911 happens that causes you to think completely different about the world around us.

In this book we will go through the basic steps to becoming more aware about these scenarios, some of the different acronyms you will hear, where to start preparing and how to do it without getting overwhelmed with all the information out there, and putting a plan and a budget in place. After that we'll go over how to start building your supplies and skills.

Think of your journey to preparedness like walking into a library, when you first walk in all you see are shelves full of books and you have no idea where to start. Knowing where to start can be a critical time saving and money saving step. This book will help remove some confusion and help you figure out what you need to learn now and what you can put on the back burner for later.

Just in time learning is crucial because we don't want to put the cart before the horse. It really does you no good to research the best long term food storage if you don't already have a few weeks' worth of food stored that you eat every day. Well go into why you should store what you eat and eat what you store later in this book.

The fact that you chose to look into prepping and self-sufficiency show you are ready to take personal responsibility for your safety and survival. You will hear about all the tools and supplies you need, but to me mindset is the most important part of prepping. Knowing that no one cares about your survival more than you and you cannot depend on someone else to "bail you out" when the going gets rough.

As preppers we need to look at the complete picture, prioritize the threats we feel are the most pertinent to our situation and prepare accordingly. We need to make sure we are staying focused on the big picture and not put all of our energy into one area like food storage and forget about having clean drinking water because 3 months' worth of food will do you no good if you only have enough water to last a week.

As I said, this book we will not only go over how to budget and plan for small and large scale disasters, but also how make a list and start to build your stockpile of supplies, always start small and work your way up, and keep in mind that everyone's situation is different. The supplies you need depend on your situation. And most importantly, keeping your preps even. Like I said, it does no good to have a year's worth of food stored if you have 1 months' worth of water.

Food water and shelter are the most important aspects of prepping, you might have heard the rule of threes, you can go 3 weeks without food, three days without water, 3 hours without shelter and 3 minutes without air. This may seem pretty basic but it's a good rule to go by when you're building your supplies. Food water and shelter are the most important aspects of prepping, if you don't have any one of these you are in for a tough time.

We all know why food and water are important but shelter sometimes gets overlooked because we all have homes so that part is taken care of right? Not really, we need to look at situations that could arise that require us to find shelter, build shelter or defend our shelter.

Food storage can be tricky depending on your living situation and storage space, it can also be tough staying organized and keeping your food from expiring. I'll share what we have learned and also some resources to point you in the right direction.

Water seems like an easy one but that couldn't be farther from the truth. All water is not clean water and we need to know how to not only store water but have the knowledge to filter and purify water. Everything else you do becomes obsolete if you don't have water.

So we'll go into some detail about all 3 of these areas in this book and help you get a little more comfortable about where you should start.

We will also go over how to organize and stay focused on the task at hand. If we don't enjoy what we are doing or we don't see the puzzle coming together, as humans we tend to get distracted and move on to something else. We can't afford to let this happen, we don't want to be the one saying "What do you mean we're out of water" or "I knew I should have kept building my preps"

The truth is, when done right prepping turns into a sort of addiction, but unlike most addictions this one could save your life.

So let's get started. But remember, take a step back, breath and think of prepping like building a house. If you don't have a good foundation to build your house on the house probably won't be standing for long, and even though duct tape is amazing, you're going to need a lot of it and some superglue to keep the walls up if you don't have a good foundation.

Everyone has different reasons for prepping and everyone has a different set of criteria to consider when starting this journey, so therefore there is no "one way" to be prepared and there is not "one type" of prepper. We are all different and we all need to tailor the way we prepare to our individual needs.

My advice to anyone just getting interested in prepping and self-sufficiency, take a step back and breathe. Yes, there are some pretty scary thing going on in the world today, that's why we are here right? But if we start off on the wrong foot we could end up wasting money and time in areas that we just don't need to at this point.

If you have a good foundation to build on you will find yourself in a much better situation a year from now than you will if you just start building that underground bunker and hiding in a hole waiting for the end.

You can't run until you learn how to walk

This book will start by explaining how to get yourself ready for any kind of disaster scenario from personal disasters to a complete collapse. All of this starts with mindset and taking account of our personal situation, like the saying goes "you can't run until you learn how to walk" and there is no reason to have thousands of dollars of supplies that you don't know how to use or was all built on debt.

Let me be honest here, if you are looking for a book that teaches about how to survive a zombie apocalypse or a book that scares you into thinking the world is ending tomorrow, this is probably not the book for you. The reality is you can't start half way through a movie and truly understand what it is all about, if you jump into the middle of a battlefield without the proper training you are not going to last long.

If you are looking for a book that will help you survive anything and are willing to start from ground zero and ready to figure out a plan that works best for you and your family, then you're in the right place. We need to take a logical look at a sometimes illogical world and formulate a plan that gives us the best possible chance for survival.

We all need to start somewhere, none of us just woke up one day and had it all figured out. But the good news is that prepping and self-sufficiency are not as complex as some people make it out to be. It's a personal decision we have all made, and a decision that takes continual and gradual improvement over time.

Before we get into the meat and potatoes of the book I would like to thank everyone in our prepping community on Facebook (you know who you are) along with others who have given me encouragement and the ability to brainstorm with you all.

No one knows everything, and if they tell you they do, you would be wise to question their motives.

Be Ready For Anything

In my opinion we cannot just be worried about an EMP or an economic collapse, we need to be ready for it all. And although there are some things that concern us more than others we don't want to be looking in one direction and get blindsided by something unexpected. We need to prioritize the events we feel are most concerning to us and prepare for those, and always have the other disaster scenarios in the back of our mind.

Ultimately if we are preparing for a small scale event like a natural disaster we will find that we are becoming more prepared for an event that will take down the entire country. This book is no different, we will start with the basic fundamentals and work our way up to becoming more self-sufficient, more aware and prepared to face any situation that might present itself in the future.

In the next chapter we get into some of the things that concern us all these days and some things that you are more concerned about because of your personal situation. Let's take a step back and look at our situation realistically and with a level head, after all the reason we prepare is so the end of the world doesn't become the end of the world.

Chapter 1 - The Real Black Friday

"We shall draw from the heart of suffering itself the means of inspiration and survival."

Winston Churchill

Every year, the Friday after Thanksgiving millions of people rush out before dawn in order to get the best deals, and find the perfect gifts for Christmas for their friends and loved ones. They trample each other, bursting through the doors of the store hoping to be the first one to the best deals the store has to offer. There is pushing, pulling, rude behavior, and everyone is out for themselves. They are not thinking about the mother they just stepped on to get to the top requested item on every child's Christmas list. A frenzy ensues as there is only so many of the one thing that everyone wants.

It Just Got Real

Now put a twist on the above scenario, only this is not black Friday, this is a few minutes after the local news reports the inevitable has finally happened, and the dollar has collapsed. Panic sets in, and everyone rushes to the grocery store or local Wal-Mart to gather food and the supplies they will need to get their family through the now hard times.

If you are brave enough to go to the store, you will see the ultimate frenzy that would rival even the largest black Friday sale. People will be buying everything in the store, EVERYTHING will be gone. The shelves will be empty, and people's carts will be full. The lines will be long, and there may even be people outside of the store ready to take everything that was just bought. People will get desperate, and do desperate things.

And It Just Gets Worse

Three days later, the stores are empty, and those who have not planned will try to hunker down, and make do with what they have, maybe. True desperation will not have truly set in yet, but it is getting worse. There is a mood of despair and anger thick in the air as people try to figure out their next step.

A week later, people will probably start to get a little more desperate. They will be hungry, and their families are hungry. Lines of people wait at the grocery store, hoping they will open their doors soon, so they can hopefully get enough food to last another week. But what they aren't expecting is the cost on everything has tripled. Supply and demand and greed is now in full force, and the masses can't afford food, so now they will try to take it. Riots will happen, shootings will become more prevalent as will home invasions. There will still be the thugs who try to steal things like TV's and video games, but more likely will be those who are simply trying to survive, and put their children to bed with a full belly.

The above scenario may or may not come true, but if we have learned anything from history we know it has before. This may be a worst case scenario of what will happen, or it could be a very mild version, only time will tell. But what you need to be thinking about now is what you should be doing to prepare and take yourself and your family out of this equation and avoid the chaos.

When the dollar collapses, notice I say when, not if, people will still have jobs, business will remain open to some extent, and there will still be utilities. Most likely a complete SHTF where everything stops working and people stop going to work won't happen. There may be huge cuts to business with thousands of jobs lost, and prices will increase, but society will still continue in some form or another. This is what you should be planning for now.

Will Work For Food

Will you still get up and go to "work" or will you need to go out and find "work"? Will your kids still go to school? And will the lights still be on in your home? How you go about your average day may drastically change. Instead of focusing on what type of emergency could happen, you should be thinking ok, something catastrophic has just happened, how am I going to handle it? You should be planning for this now. Start with recognizing where you are now in your planning, and where you would like to be. Stop thinking about what if, and start planning for it now.

In an economic or partial economic collapse, tangible goods will be difficult if not impossible to get. So start purchasing extras now. Buy extra every time you go to the grocery store. Instead of buying one box of instant mashed potatoes, buy two. Do the same with canned goods, cereals and pasta. Stock up on these pantry items until you have enough food for your family for at least three months. You can do the same with freezer foods, however if your power is interrupted, you may lose what you have stored in the freezer. You can plan for this by having a generator, or learn how to can things like meat and meals. Canning is a very good option if done properly.

Being Prepared

By having a well-stocked pantry, if things take a turn for the worst, you won't find yourself running to the grocery store with the masses. Hopefully you will be able to ride out the economic down turn with what you have on hand. By having a well-stocked pantry, you won't have to face that last ditch effort of getting everything you can. You can stay at home, and maybe consider hiding some of your stores. If it gets bad, you don't want stranger to come in and take what you have been working so hard to stockpile. It may be a little "zombie apocalypse" so to speak, but do you really want to take that chance? If someone were to break into your home when you weren't there, hiding your cache throughout your home may give you enough food to get through the tough times. So stock up on items you use and hide them in plain sight throughout your home, hide them in places that people would not think about looking. Going through your kitchen cabinets will be the first place people will search, but what about creating a hidden pantry in a closet, or under your bed? Those that have been prepping will know areas of where to look in your home, but the odds are in your favor that some random looter isn't going to search under your bed or behind the pots and pans for canned goods.

Building Community

However, when things change, and people start to become desperate, you should plan for them to want what you have. One of the best was to deal with this is to have a good relationship with those who live around you. A small community of likeminded individuals will fare better than those who are only out for themselves. Talk to your neighbors. Make it a point to say hi, and strike up a conversation. Does your next door neighbor have a great garden? Go ask them what they are doing to have such a bountiful harvest. Become an active participant in your community. This will keep you aware of what is going on around you, as well as meet your neighbors and learn what their concerns are. Everyone has something useful to offer and will have some sort of skills. By working together, and having a same general goal, a community is better than trying to get through this on your own. Safety in numbers is very appropriate for this type of scenario, and if your neighbors are looking out for you and vice versa, you have just increased your odds that your family will get through this. And being able to discuss and plan with likeminded individuals will help your general sense of wellbeing.

Your Most Important Tool Is Sitting On Your Shoulders

Perhaps the most important aspect of survival is your mindset. In any type of crisis situation, keeping a level head can mean the difference between life and death. Ok, that may be a little dramatic, but it's true. By really accepting that something can happen that will change the way you live your life, and doing things now to prepare you have taken the very important step of preparing yourself and your family for the inevitable. Realize that this will happen, and have a plan in place. Start living that way

now, don't wait to start tomorrow. Keep a level head, and don't get sucked into what the mass media is feeding you. When something does happen, remain calm, and go forward with your day in the same way you have been, in a prepared frame of mind.

Why we need to put away your comfy little house slippers and wake up to reality

It seems like everyone has their heads buried in the sand. If you close your eyes the monster doesn't exist right? I'm here to tell you, that monster does exist! If you look under your bed you will see that monster disguised as freedom. And that "monster" is going to take all of your defenses, all of our liberties and make you feel all cozy and nice inside until it finally has you in a position where you have no choice but to do as it says.

Every day we get closer and closer to that situation. Why do you think the government wants to open up the border? Why is the government so willing to give illegal aliens the same rights as **we the people** born and raised in this country?

Because they are easy to control and willing to do what the government asks. The government needs to get bigger, they don't see how close an economic collapse is. And if they do they want nothing to do with changing it...because life is good on the hill.

It's simple: The more people who live in this country that rely on the government for handouts, welfare, food stamps and a million of other money wasting programs THAT WE PAY FOR the more they feel like they can spend. I mean the national debt is only 17 trillion right? We can afford to spend a few million researching the research we are doing to see if a water Lilly can survive above timberline. And as long as these people get their monthly check from the government they don't give a damn what the government spends OUR money on.

I am no conspiracy theorist by any means, I do believe we actually landed on the moon. But I do know that where there's smoke there's fire...and there's no smoke anymore, everything is on fire. It is truly only a matter of time before the S hits the fan and everyone has to uncover their eyes and admit the THIS IS NOT A DREAM. Will this happen in our life time? Maybe, maybe not. But are you willing to take that chance? I'm not! And that is why I started the Survivalist Prepper website, for me to vent and to inform anyone interested in learning the facts.

This book will help you become a better prepper and more educated about what is really going on around the world. There are a hundred different things that could happen tomorrow that could change our lives forever, and while you cannot possibly be prepared for every situation you need to be as ready as we can for anything.

I am a God fearing man, and I believe that if he wants something to happen it is going to happen...period, but like Benjamin Franklin said I also believe the God helps those who help themselves and if there is anything I can do to ensure the survival of my family I think it is my responsibility to do so.

My point is, who knows what is going to happen and no one really knows when. Being prepared for any disaster is just like car insurance, I don't want to get in an accident; but if I do, I would feel a lot better knowing I am not going to have to pay for it in the future.

The Unprepared Will Panic - The Prepared Will Survive.

It is natural for some people to panic when confronted with a crisis. Most are not prepared mentally or physically for a disaster situation, and are immediately overwhelmed, and in some cases cannot function. People panic because they do not know what to do next. Flight or fight, the emotions swirl in peoples' minds and people are, without actually realizing it, deciding whether to confront the matter emotionally (fight) or deny it (flight) and some cannot not make any decisions at all, decisions that may save lives.

Given the state of the world and the country today, it is only a matter of time. It is not a matter of if, but simply of when a hacker slips through the firewalls and shuts down the power grid or a nuclear device is detonated in the heart of some city. It could also be a natural disaster of such magnitude that it shuts down large portions of the country for months or even years.

What Can You Expect As a Prepper

Surviving the disaster itself is one thing but surviving the affects of it is another. The days, weeks, and possibly even years after will dwarf the actual event as far as devastation and turmoil and will have a greater affect on people psychologically.

The first few days' people will naturally assume it is temporary and most will convince themselves they can manage until the authorities sort things out. After three to five days have passed, people begin stirring and wondering. They may gather to trade gossip and some people would have already tried to contact the local government. As soon as the citizens realize the crisis is unlike any they have ever experienced they will call on the government for help and when they realize help is not forthcoming, they will turn against the government.

The Unprepared People

Those that relied on others for their daily sustenance before the crisis will likely have to rely on others after the crisis, they are used to asking, and for the most part, they are not a threat at this point.

Then there are those that never really asked for help but simply are not prepared for the crisis, as far as supplies, knowledge and skill sets go. They only know how to survive when the rules have been established and everyone plays their part. Show up for work at nine and leave at five, a paycheck twice a month, a routine they fell into because it is all they know.

This group will become a threat because they know they cannot survive without rules and some form of governance, they know what they know but have not expanded beyond their bubble. They will become desperate quickly and will seek out those that appear to be in charge, and usually will fall prey to those with an agenda and of those taking advantage of the crisis. Instigators and anarchist will find and use these people for demonstrations and most will march and clamor with no idea what they are demonstrating against.

Then there are those that have been paying attention, they knew something was coming and they prepared because they realized that depending on others is not a wise move. They work hard and want to be left alone to survive as only they know how. They know what they need to do, and will continue to do it. No one will stop them from surviving...These people are you and I.

The Lights Are Out For Good

The entire world runs on electricity and essentially any type of disaster can cause the lights to stay out for years. Terrorist organizations and rouge nations know all they have to do is shut the lights off and the country comes to a halt. The financial markets will collapse, transportation hubs will shut down and manufacturing will stop. Electricity is the keystone that keeps the country from collapsing.

People will panic, and race in circles instead of stopping to evaluate the situation. They know deep in their minds they made a mistake, by not being prepared, denial is not possible now but there is no going back.

They have families and they will be a threat to everyone, because they will turn to violence, thievery and deception all in the name of providing for their families. They can be your neighbors, friends or strangers. You have no idea how your neighbors or friends may react because you have nothing to compare it too.

What You Can Do As a Prepper?

Knowledge and knowing how to apply that knowledge will prevent you and others from essentially "freaking" out during a crisis. The first thing to keep in mind is it is not necessarily the disaster itself you need to prepare for but the affects of the disaster. Focusing on a singular event may cause some to overlook the fact that regardless of the crisis, there is always going to be the days after and they will be the hardest to survive.

Training is important, and it must be done in a controlled environment so you can learn from your mistakes without costing lives. Once a calamity is upon you training is over, and then the application of everything you know comes into play.

Reading about Prepping and preparing on the Internet is a starting point but again, you must know how to apply what you are learning. For example, you may understand the theory behind a magnesium stick and how it makes fire but you must also learn the mechanics by doing it yourself. If you know what to do next, you will not panic, and the only way to know what to do is to practice.

What to Be Prepared For

The reality of the situation is that you will not have as many supplies as you think, so another reality is that you cannot afford to give any away. Rarely can anyone accurately calculate amounts needed for a specific period. You can get an estimate but always err on the side of caution. If you firmly believe you have a year's supply of food, you should assume you only have a nine-month's supply. Waste, damage, spoilage and any number of other factors will reduce your supplies and among them is giving to friends and others or having your supplies stolen.

Avoid making any alliances in the first few weeks or months. People will naturally seek out others for comfort or material things. Once a few months have passed those that have survived, know how to survive and will not be as a big of a threat to you.

False leaders will emerge in your community and will pray on the weaknesses and fear of those suffering. There will always be those ready to take advantage of any crisis. Con artists will move among people making promises. So-called black-markets will spring up where food and water stolen and looted from others will be on sale.

Once you realize the magnitude of the crisis, it will be time to seek out those that have skills that can be used to rebuild society. You will need carpenters, doctors and engineers, as well as farmers and other agricultural experts. Even if the crisis is only for a few months society will change, and having a skill that is useful to the community will make you a valuable resource.

Stress in a SHTF Scenario

As we prepare ourselves and our family for an impending economic collapse or natural disaster we are constantly thinking about how much water we need or how long we can survive if the lights were out for an extended period of time. One thing that is just as important as all of that is your mental wellbeing and dealing with stress in a SHTF scenario, It's not just about how you will react during the beginning stages of a disaster, but how will the affects of a disaster wear you down mentally over time.

Turn the Lights Out

A way I have tried to see how my family would react without having what we think we need on a daily basis is simulate an off the grid event by shutting the power off for 24 hours. Although this does not tell you exactly how someone will react it will give you some small clues that will tell you how they could possibly react when the real thing happens.

Keep in mind that not being able to flush the toilet for 24 hours is far less stressful than not being able to flush the toilet and having to figure out how to remove the waste from your home, come to think of it I don't think anyone went #2 that night.

Some things I learned about my family that night were...

1. In the beginning it was all fun and games, until slowly you begin to realize how many things we do and take for granted that you are not able to do without power.

2. Frustration becomes a bigger issue as the day goes on, the children run out of things to keep them busy and "get bored" very quickly

3. When the sun goes down and the realization that the lights are not coming on sets in (especially to the children) and you begin to see how bad it could be if you had to do this every day, and you have plenty of time to think about how you would adjust.

4. On a positive note it gives you the opportunity to bond with your family without all of the other everyday distraction and discuss what you would do if there was no power for months, because you basically have a "captive" audience.

I wouldn't suggest doing this unless you and your spouse are both on board, you might end up with less money to spend on preps because you are spending it all on a lawyer...just saying.

The Beginning Stages of Stress

In the beginning stages of any off the grid event or disaster you will not have as much time to think and react as we do now, this is why prepping is so important and is not just about stockpiling food and water. Take a look at yourself and ask yourself "how well

do I handle tough situations?" The odds are you are giving yourself too much credit.

In some cases people would become just like heroin addict or alcoholics, willing to do whatever it takes to get what they need, and willing to hurt anyone they have to in order to get what they need. Have you ever gone the whole day without eating? As the day goes on that is all you think about, and at some point this becomes your first priority. Now just imagine how that would be if you had no food, and you had to figure something out quick to ensure your survival. What would you do?

Trying times can bring out the best in people; it can also bring out the worst. If criminals know that there are no police around to stop them, they're job just got a little easier, and the people who do not commit crimes only refrain from it because of the threat of prosecution.

On the other hand most people tend to band together, create communities and work together for a common goal. Hopefully we become these people, and hopefully we are prepared to defend ourselves not only physically but mentally as well.

As time goes on there will be two types of criminals you will need to be ready for, the people that are just wired that way, and the people who become that way out of desperation.

Desperate people could be more dangerous in this situation for two reasons.

1. Because they will be just that, desperate, and as a result be willing to do whatever it takes to get what they need to survive.

2. because it would be easier for us to justify defending ourselves against a "bad" person than it would to justify having to injure or harm a desperate woman with a child that is willing to kill you to feed her family.

The Effects of Traumatic Events

Traumatic situation have a way of changing people, we see this all the time with our soldier who fight in wars or are involved in a stressful environment for long periods of time, it's called Post Traumatic Stress Disorder (P.T.S.D.) We could possibly face the same traumatic events that causes this disorder if our infrastructure were to crumble and crime death and chaos were to become part of our everyday lives.

How would you react if seeing dead bodies or seeing people get killed became a part of your daily life? At first you be horrified by this, but eventually you would become desensitized to the situation because it became a part of the world you lived in. Some people handle this stress better than others, but in some way or another it would affect all of us.

In the beginning stages of any catastrophic event shock and denial are typical human reactions. In an article from the American Psychological Association they explain what happens to people after a disaster or other catastrophic event this way...

Shock and denial are typical responses to traumatic events and disasters, especially shortly after the event. Both shock and denial are normal protective reactions.

Shock is a sudden and often intense disturbance of your emotional state that may leave you feeling stunned or dazed. Denial involves not acknowledging that something very stressful has happened, or not experiencing fully the intensity of the event. You may temporarily feel numb or disconnected from life.

As the initial shock subsides, reactions vary from one person to another. The following, however, are normal responses to a traumatic event:

• Feelings become intense and sometimes are unpredictable. You may become more irritable than usual, and your mood may change back and forth dramatically. You might be especially anxious or nervous, or even become depressed.

• Thoughts and behavior patterns are affected by the trauma. You might have repeated and vivid memories of the event. These flashbacks may occur for no apparent reason and may lead to physical reactions such as rapid heartbeat or sweating. You may find it difficult to concentrate or make decisions, or become more easily confused. Sleep and eating patterns also may be disrupted.

• Recurring emotional reactions are common. Anniversaries of the event, such as at one month or one year, can trigger upsetting memories of the traumatic experience. These "triggers" may be accompanied by fears that the stressful event will be repeated.

• Interpersonal relationships often become strained. Greater conflict, such as more frequent arguments with family members and coworkers, is common. On the other hand, you might become withdrawn and isolated and avoid your usual activities.

• Physical symptoms may accompany the extreme stress. For example, headaches, nausea and chest pain may result and may require medical attention. Pre-existing medical conditions may worsen due to the stress.

Long Term Stress

After that shock and denial subside it does not mean the worst is over. In the event of any long term disaster there will be no doctors or psychiatrist to help you work through this, and on top of that the problems are not going away, they have just become different problem.

As a SHTF situation becomes more long term it becomes a reality you need to face and adapt to in order to survive. Decisions we would have made 6 months ago might not be an option today, and how we handle stress or how mentally stable we are at that point could cause us to make completely different decision, possibly justifying a very bad decision.

It really is hard to tell how someone will react or deal with stress during a disaster scenario and that is why they say "trust no one" you never know what even the most respected and trustworthy individual will do if they are affected by psychological problems or situations that require them to make decisions they would not have made if everything was "normal.

Chapter 2 - Cause And Effect – Security

"Shallow men believe in luck or in circumstance. Strong men believe in cause and effect."

Ralph Waldo Emerson

Operational Security and Basic Home Security

Securing your preps and protecting yourself from anyone who wants what you have is not something you should do just in case the S hits TF, it is something you should already be doing. There are plenty of reasons why this is important today, and plenty of people who are will to take what you have if you are going to make it easy for them.

Securing your home shouldn't start from inside your home, it should start at the outside edge of your property working in. By working outside in you will potentially increase the time between you being alerted to an intruder to the time when you need to either face the intruder or escape. Every second counts and anything you can do to make it even just a little bit harder to enter your home will give you those few precious seconds you need to react.

Basic home security could be the difference between someone passing your home up and going to the next house, so start by looking around your home and put yourself in the intruder's shoes, what would you do if you had to get in. As a teenager I had to break into my own home a couple of times after school, if you have kids ask them "how would you get in?" Now not all teenagers are criminals but they will be less concerned about property damage than you, after all they don't have to pay to get it fixed...you do, so by doing this you might get a different point of view.

Simple things like keeping the doors and windows locked and the bushes outside your windows trimmed to take away hiding spots for intruders would make it harder for an intruder to get in. Criminals are opportunists and criminals take the path of least resistance, they weigh risk and reward just like we do, but while we risk driving through rush hour for our weekly pay check, they risk jail time for an easy payday.

Anyone who wants to get through a door or window bad enough will do so regardless what you do, but what you can do to make it a little tougher for them is make sure you have good locks...and use them and they even make film you can put on your windows that will stop the windows from shattering (kind of like window tint) And again, this won't stop someone who wants in badly enough, but it could give you a few extra seconds to defend yourself.

Also make sure you have adequate lighting around the exterior of your house. Look around and find the blind spots and purchase lights to remove the areas someone could hide.

Inside your home is also important, get a timer for when you are not home and have the lights come on a certain times and give the appearance you are there. Most criminals are looking to get in and out and do not want to hurt you physically, they just want your toys.

Alarms

Alarms are great to have if you can afford it, but there are other low cost options available other than Brinks home security. Something as simple as Christmas bells over doorways could give you a little advance warning of unwelcome visitors and possibly give them a little scare and startle them away.

A solar driveway sensor or even a battery powered motion sensor are great to have because if there is no power you still get warning if someone comes up your driveway. If your house is tucked back from the street or you live in a rural area you can't depend on your neighbors to know if someone is breaking into your home and although a motion sensor will not alert your neighbors, it would alert you if you happen to be home if someone tries to break in, giving you time to get out of harm's way, call the authorities or do what you have to do at that point.

Dummy cams are another alternative to expensive home security systems. You can find dummy cams for as little as $20 for a set of 4. Again this will not stop someone who is dead set on getting into your home, but if they see these above your front and back doors they will think twice about entering your home.

Non-lethal Weapons and Self Defense

Let's go over self-defense and non-lethal weapons you can use around your home. Keep in mind that I am not stating that a stun gun or pepper spray should be an absolute alternative to a fire arm, I am saying that it is always good to have other options available when you can't get to your firearm or when the situation presents itself that does not require lethal force.

Another aspect to consider when thinking about pepper spray vs a fire are is that you can't have 5 guns laying around the house because it's just not safe. But you can however have cans of pepper spray strategically placed around your home like under a table or window sill fastened with Velcro, in drawers or even hanging from your front door knob.

pepper spray or even a stun gun are close contact weapons, this is why they can never take the place of a firearm, you can potentially "defuse" a situation from a distance with a firearm, but someone has to be close enough to physically injure you if you are using a stun gun or pepper spray. And remember, extracting yourself from a potentially violent situation is always preferred unless there is no other option.

Look in the Mirror

Now that we've talked about securing your perimeter and your home let's take a look at you. What is that you do on a daily basis that puts you at risk? Or gives someone a reason to feel like they can take what you have?

Are you one of those people who have to brag about their new toys? Are you one of those people that leave your car door open while you're pumping gas? Or are you one of those people that always go to the bank straight after work on payday? The truth is we have all probably been guilty of this at one point or another but these are the simple things we can try to avoid that make us a target.

Don't go out to lunch and tell your friend about that new 90" television you just bought, they might not come steal it, but the guy behind you listening in on your conversation might.

Or you could tell your best friend about your new generator in the garage and they could talk to other people increasing the chances that the wrong person finds out about a new toy they can get for free.

And along with bragging, don't put your house on display. The more you fly under the radar and the more your home looks like a waste of time to an intruder the more likely they will be to move to the next home.

Don't leave your garage open for everyone to see what you have. I don't know how many times I drive through a suburban neighborhood and see every other house with the garage door open showing how many motorcycles or bikes they have, not to mention that brand new set of golf clubs sitting in the corner.

Something else you should do is always know your surroundings and what poses the biggest threat. Get to know your neighbors and you will find out who the ones that are going to help you protect your home, and the ones who you need to protect your home against.

Jack Spirko of the survival podcast put it very simple, perform an "Am I being stupid audit" If we constantly leave the garage door open, or we always go directly to the bank after work on payday

or we have a wad of cash sticking out of our back pocket, well…
we are being stupid and we need to fix that because people are
already looking for a reasons to come take what we have, and we
don't need to be the ones who give them that reason.

Taking a Personal Audit of Your Situation

Taking a personal audit should consist of two categories, what
disaster scenarios concern you the most and what can you do to
put yourself in a position to get ready for those situations. So by
using the Cause and Effect worksheet on the resources page we
can figure out what situations we should be preparing for now
and what situations we can work towards becoming prepared for
in the future. Let's do a little experiment, fill out the Cause and
effect worksheet now, and then fill it out again after you read the
next section. You might have a clearer head the second time
around.

Preparedness Planning and Prioritizing

Ok, so you need at least 5 years' worth of food stored and not
only do you need to store 5 thousand gallons of water you need
to also have a water catchment system in place for when you run
out. And don't forget that you need a bug out bag for every
member of your family, a lights out kit, a generator and or a
battery bank, a car safety kit, a first aid kit that covers everything
from a small scratch to a severed leg. Oh yeah, bug in bags just in
case everyone in your home are in different places, a few caches
set up along the way to your bug out location that needs to be
stocked with even more water, food and weapons which you
should have no problem getting to once you have at least 100
gallons of fuel stored.

So where do you start because everything is going downhill fast
and you need all of this stuff by the end of the month. What
about getting a few more credit cards and maxing them out?

What about quitting your job and cashing out your 401K? You could possibly even sell the house because when the poop hits the fan in a month everything is going to be worthless anyway right?

Stop! Let's take a step back and breathe. Hopefully right now you are saying "who the hell is this guy?" and "that doesn't sound like a very good plan to me!" But if the thought is spinning around your head right now saying "yeah, why not? Just imagine how much extra money I would have and how much gold I could buy!" you need to take a step back and put your wallet back in your pocket because everything is probably going to be ok for a while.

If we were absolutely certain that it will be the end of the world as we know it in 30 days, and by absolutely certain I mean that you saw on the news that an asteroid the size of a football field is going to hit Mexico and were all hosed. Well in that case sure, do what you have to do. But if you are not absolutely certain that the world is going to be turned upside down you might want to take a different approach.

The smart thing to do is to have a plan and take baby steps, the truth is that something could very well happen next week, but what if it doesn't? And what if you dug yourself a hole too big to get out of and you now less prepared than you were in the first place. Sure you have all the supply's you need but you can't pay your rent so you need to sell everything you just bought at a fraction of what you paid for it.

Now this probably seems a little extreme but it illustrates the point that when we first become interested in the preparedness mindset we are inundated with all of this information. This is because everyone is at a different level of preparedness and everyone has certain needs and concerns they need to fulfill.

This is why we need to create a good plan of action and build a good foundation that helps us slowly move in the right direction. By creating a plan we can define where we need to start rather than saying "well I need to start somewhere so I guess I'll go buy some solar panels and a shotgun"

It makes no sense to go out and buy a shotgun if you have no idea about firearm safety, and it makes no sense to go out and buy $500 worth of long term food if you only have 10 gallons of water stored.

We need to look at being prepared as a time period and not as a supply list. By starting with the basics and preparing for a small scale disaster that would only last a few days or a week we can keep our preps even and make sure we have all of our bases covered for that week and work our way up to being prepared for a month, 6 months, a year and so on.

Prioritize Your Threats and Needs

So where do we start? Like I said everyone has different priorities and different circumstances they are restricted by. Your living situation, location, age and family makeup all play a factor when you are putting together your plan. So we need to formulate a plan that works for us and our family, not just do what everyone else is doing.

If you live in an apartment you probably won't be able to own chickens and the way you store food and water are going to be different than someone with 10 acres of property. And your bug out plans will be different if you live in an urban area than they will be if you live in a rural area.

Start by making a personalized plan centered on what your concerns and needs are and start there. You can use the worksheet in the links below to get a better idea about what concerns you the most and how prepared you are for that scenario right now. This might seem a little simple and you might be thinking "I already know what I am concerned about" but you might be surprised by the results and find out that you are either more prepared than you thought you were, or you have more work that you thought you did.

What Do Those Threats Mean to You?

Once you define what threats are the most concerning to you and your family you will need to define what those threats mean to you. How long will they last? What do you need to do to increase your chances of survival during that crisis? What special needs do you and your family have that needs to be taken into consideration?

For example, some people feel like an economic collapse will cause the complete failure of society. The grid will be down, there will be riots in the streets and the government will enact martial law. Others believe it will be a slow gradual decline causing hyperinflation and job loss. And some people just want to be prepared for a natural disaster that is likely in their area.

As you define what these threats mean, you will begin the process of narrowing down the long list in the beginning to something more manageable and more focused on your individual needs, and as you begin building you supplies and food storage you will have a better idea about what you need now, and what can wait until a little bit later.

Another factor to consider is bugging in or bugging out. How you define these threats will probably determine which direction you need to go and what supplies you need to have to become more prepared. If you live in a rural area you might not be as concerned about bugging out, if you live downtown next door to a Walmart you might want to have an escape plan or 2 ready and practice those plans regularly.

As you define these threats you also need to take into consideration your family and what threats they feel are the most probable. Their point of view might be a little different than yours and having everyone on the same page will only help during your journey to preparedness.

Unfortunately some people just don't want to be bothered with this and some people are forced to do this on their own. This could be because some people don't want to look at the situations we face realistically because it scares them too much, or someone is willing to roll the dice that nothing is going to happen and some people will just think you are flat out crazy.

This is another reason why is smart to start small and work your way up. These people are far more likely to "appease" you if you explain that you just want to be ready if the power goes out for a few days. And as you begin to become more prepared hopefully the light goes on in their head and they say "this really isn't that crazy after all"

Your Personal and Family Needs

As you are defining these threats you also need to take into consideration any special family needs you might have and what limitations you might encounter because of your family makeup. Your food storage plans will be different if you have an infant than they will be if it's just you and your spouse, and your bug out plans will be different if you have someone in your house hold that is elderly or disabled.

Regardless of your family make up the basics are the same, you need to have a well thought out plan and be ready for anything that might occur in the future. Even if your entire family is not on board with what you are doing you still need a plan in place that insures their safety, it's just a little easier to do if they are.

If something happens and your family is separated have a plan in place where everyone knows where to go and what to do. And Like I said earlier the way you pose this scenario to them is crucial. If you say "if a nuclear bomb hits downtown and I'm at work and you are at school we need to meet at our bug out location because that's where the radiation suits are" you're going to get that look from them, you know that look right?

But if you let them know that you want to have a plan just in case anything were to happen you want to make sure everyone knows where to meet and what needs to be done to get the family back together in one place. Most teenagers will probably give you that look anyway, but when it comes down to it they will remember and probably glad they have crazy parents.

Family Communication

Communicating with your family while they are separated might not be as easy as sending a text message or calling them, if the grid is down and cell phones are not working your family will need to know where and what to do beforehand. This is why it's important to have a plan beforehand and make sure everyone is on the same page.

Another thing to consider is having your important documents in one place and having copies of these important documents in an emergency kit and ready to go just in case you need them to find your family. These documents could be pictures, social security cards, birth certificates, medical records or anything that would help identify your loved one.

A Quick Recap

Remember, you don't need everything right now. The chances are we are never going to be fully prepared for every possible scenario and by going into further debt buying supplies and items we feel are necessary we are not guaranteeing our survival, all we are doing is guaranteeing we won't be able to do what we need to do in the future.

So take small steps at first and those small steps will turn into you becoming more prepared in no time at all. If we build a good foundation and keep our preps even along the way we can save ourselves from wasting valuable dollars and time along the way.

Define these threats and define what they mean to you will also save you time and money along the way to becoming more prepared. If you're more worried about an EMP than a pandemic then you should probably wait to buy that gas mask and work on learning about faraday cages and how to live without electricity or make your own.

And remember the reason we all do this is our survival and the survival of our family's so proper planning is critical and doesn't cost a dime. And as a matter of fact I would suggest that in the first month or so you focus on the basics like planning and prioritizing and not buy anything at all, because it usually turns out that you buy something you thought you needed and once you become more educated about preparing you find out that you probably didn't really need that brand new solar cell phone charger as much as you thought you did.

Our geographic location and our financial situation will play the biggest role when it comes to where you start preparing and how long it will take to become more comfortable with your current situation. Understanding that the end of the world doesn't have to be the end of the world if we are prepared to handle it is the place every prepper should start. Knowing what disaster situation is most likely to affect you, planning for those events and seeing the big picture will not only help you survive any of the smaller events, but you will find that as you prepare for those events you are becoming more prepared for the larger events like an economic collapse.

Chapter 3 - Possible Disaster Scenarios

"The tree of liberty must be refreshed from time to time with the blood of patriots and tyrants."

Thomas Jefferson

Here is a brief overview of some of the disaster scenarios that could affect you in the future. Keep these in mind as you read through this book, and if needed come back to review them when you fill out your cause and effect worksheet.

Economic Collapse

This could be one of the biggest issues we face as Americans today; an economic collapse could cause a chain reaction that leads to other doomsday scenarios like a police state, long term off the grid event or the complete collapse of the infrastructure like we see in Detroit today.

An economic collapse is inevitable, and when this happens the soft content people that this government has created will look to them for guidance to survive a problem that that very same government caused. I don't think there is a way to stop this locomotive from going off the cliff, I think the only thing we can do is prepare to fight for our freedoms just as our founding fathers did.

In the case of an economic collapse your life will be turned upside down. The paper that your money is printed on will be just that, paper. If you have done a good job prepping, most of your possessions will be more valuable than any printed money, and even gold.

Drinkable water, food and supplies you have prepped would become the new gold. But having these supplies is one thing, keeping these supplies is an entirely different problem. Preparing and protecting the things you have stockpiled are crucial to your survival, no matter what situation you find yourself in.

There are some things that remain the same regardless of where you live, your money will be worthless, you will need to have an escape plan and you should have caches set up along your escape routes as an added precaution. It is always better to walk away alive and empty handed than dead and empty handed, especially if you know you have a cache of survival supplies nearby.

Police State/ Martial Law

A police state is what I consider a secondary event, a police state will be caused by a different number of events that cause the infrastructure to crumble. Anything that would cause the breakdown of our infrastructure could potentially cause a police state or give our government an excuse to enact martial law.

Off The Grid Event

An off the grid event could affect just your city or town to the entire united states. An off the grid event could be caused by an EMP, over usage of our resources, civil unrest or military conflicts. A grid down scenario could affect our daily lives down the minutest detail, we use electricity for everything from charging our phones to heating our homes in the winter.

EMP

An EMP is defined as rapidly changing electric fields and magnetic fields may couple with electrical/electronic systems to produce damaging current and voltage surges. An EMP that is large enough to affect the entire United states could possibly cause and off the grid event, followed by a police state, and causing an economic collapse (not necessarily in that order.) An EMP does not necessarily have to come from the sun, if someone has the capability to detonate a nuclear EMP warhead above the United States it could literally cripple our economy.

Terrorism

Terrorists are inventing new ways to create chaos on a daily basis, and with seemingly everyone in the world having their sights set on the Unites States this is something we should be increasingly concerned about. Terrorism is not just blowing up a building, terrorism these days means flying airplanes into buildings, planting IED's (improvised explosive device) and the most possible (in my opinion) biological warfare or bio terror.

Pandemic/Influenza

As much as we travel around the world today and how quickly we can do it a pandemic is a bigger doomsday scenario than it ever has been. An influenza virus that originates in China could make it to the United States before we even know what hit us. 1 airport could be the artery that carry's a virus around the world in hours.

It's Not Just About Doomsday

Preppers are not only preparing for EMP's or an economic collapse, some of us actually prepare for situations that could directly affect our lives like a tornado tearing down our home, an earthquake that tears a city apart, leaving us with no power and people cut off from the outside world, leaving us to fend for themselves. Which of these situations is most likely to affect you? How prepared are you if you had to survive a week with what you have in your car or your home.

Natural Disasters

Not all preppers are preparing for EMP's or an economic collapse, some of us actually prepare for situations that could directly affect our lives like a tornado tearing down our home, an earthquake that tears a city apart, leaving us with no power, chaos all around us and people cut off from the outside world leaving them to fend for themselves. Which of these situations is most likely to affect you? How prepared are you if you had to survive a week with what you have in your car or your home?

Preparing for situations like these is actually a good starting point because as you prepare for some of these more localized events, you will be preparing for other events like being off the grid without even knowing it.

The basics of preparing for a natural disaster is based on the same principal as preparing for a national event, you need to start with being able to survive for the first 3 days.

Having the right supplies really depends on what natural disaster is most likely to affect you where you live. I wrote a post about what I have in my 72 hour bag if you are looking for a starting point, but like I said your situation will define your needs.

Earthquakes

An earthquake has the potential to tear down a city, and if you are unfortunate enough to have your life affected by an earthquake that caused a city to become chaotic and cut off from the outside world because the highways and airports are destroyed you would need to be able to either sustain yourself until help arrived, or prepared enough to get out on foot, this is all assuming you were lucky enough to survive.

Some areas of this country are more susceptible to earthquakes than others, but that does not mean that because you live in Montana that an earthquake is not possible, although it is very unlikely.

There are other events that could cause the same affects as an earthquake, like bombs, civil war and riots. These are not going to tear a gaping crack through your neighborhood, but they could have you trapped in a certain area and your survival options will be somewhat similar to an earthquake, can you ride the storm out or can you get out of dodge safely.

Earthquake Survival Basics:

- Look for something sturdy to hide under, Stay away from windows or anything else that could fall and injure you and always cover your head.

- Stay in one spot until the earthquake is completely over

- Brace any fixtures like pictures and heavy cabinets to the wall, including water heaters and gas appliances to avoid gas leaks. Make sure everyone knows where the gas shut off is.

- Always have a first aid kit and emergency supplies available.

- If you are in a car, try to stay off (or get off safely) bridges and over passes or mountain roads where rock slides could occur.

- Know the earthquake escape routes of the building you are in.

- Be aware of the aftermath just because the earthquake is over does not mean all is well, there could be aftershocks, tsunamis or landslides.

Tornadoes

Tornadoes are even more localized than earthquakes, tornado's basically hit the ground, and if you are in the path of that tornado you could have everything you own tossed around for three miles in any direction.

In the event of a tornado you might not have the option to evacuate, you might need to find the safest place in your home and ride out the storm so to speak. Make sure you have a plan and your family knows what to do and where to go in the event that your home is in the path of a tornado.

Tornado Survival Basics

- Pay attention to your local weather alerts and be aware of what the sky looks like outside your front door.

- Find the lowest/safest spot in your home away from windows or possible flying debri.

- Have a safety plan and Practice it with your family so they know how to react quickly.

- Prepare your home before hand by removing anything that could become a "projectile" broken tree limbs, lawn furniture or hanging plants or fixtures.

- have any important documents, food, water and supplies stored below ground and protected from the possible tornado damage.

- Watch for dark clouds that are moving in different directions or forming funnel clouds and large hail.

Hurricane/floods/tsunami

Hurricanes and floods can cause far more damage than just destroying homes and roads. Following a major earthquake, a 15-metre tsunami disabled the power supply and cooling of three Fukushima Daiichi reactors, causing a nuclear accident on 11 March 2011. All three cores largely melted in the first three days. The point is that even if you are not worried about an earthquake or a tsunami the cause and effect of one disaster could lead to other disasters.

A hurricane or flood can literally rip a city apart, New Orleans was decimated because of a hurricane which cause faulty levy's to bust open and flood the city. There were (and still are) many people in New Orleans that were unprepared and reliant on the government for their survival, and as a result when help was slow to come it caused a chain reaction of other dangerous events and crime.

Flood Survival Basics

- Have at least 3 days of food and water, or better yet a 72 hour bag ready to go for every member of your family. For hurricanes I would suggest at least 3 week's worth of supplies.

- Have a crank radio or some way to stay up to date about the current situation.

- Be aware of the escalating situation and be prepared to evacuate at a moment's notice.

- Stay out of the water. 6 inches of fast moving water is all it takes to take a person down.

- Move to higher ground and get away from rising water.

- If you are in a car, don't try to drive through a flooded street, if it is too late, get out of the car and move to higher ground if possible.

Wildfires

Wildfires will devour anything and everything in it's path, and if that happens to be your home your best option is to get out as quickly as possible. How quickly a fire spreads depends on the weather conditions, wind direction and your climate.

There are some things you can do to mitigate the possible damage to your home or property far before a fire gets to your front door. Don't just depend on the fire department to save you home and belongings because they will already have their hands full and their first priority is saving lives.

Wildfire Survival Basics

- Have emergency phone numbers and an evacuation plan in place.

- If your kids are at school and you are at work you will need a safe location to meet up, have a location picked out beforehand.

- Prepare your home to withstand a wild fire by trimming trees 4 feet above the ground, removing any leaves or branches on the ground that could become tinder.

- Don't use materials like wood chips for flower beds around your home, this is just fuel for the fire.

- Have firefighting tool ready to go, tools like shovels, rakes and garden hoses that could help prevent a fire from consuming your house.

- Have a bug out plan. Have everything you need ready to go at a moment's notice, including important documents.

If you would like more information about how to prepare for natural disasters you can visits sites like the Red Cross and FEMA for more information

Surviving Personal Doomsdays

We hear all the time about preparing for the pending economic collapse, martial law or even an EMP, but we don't hear enough about preparing for a personal doomsday. This is probably because people love drama, people love the big doomsday stories, but the reality is that we should all start preparing on a much smaller scale while we look at the bigger picture.

I recently lost my mother and while I was sitting in the hospital room all I could think about was how the dynamics of my family were going to change if my mother made it through this. The way I prepped would change, my bug out strategies would change and how our daily lives were going to change with her living with us. Unfortunately my mother did not make it and I never had the opportunity to implement these strategies.

This got me thinking about personal doomsday scenarios that could not only affect our daily lives, but it also changes our ability to prep for bigger disasters on a daily basis. As we prepare for smaller more localized events like the loss of a job or natural disasters we are inherently on our way to being prepared for a disaster on a bigger scale.

Another factor to take into account is that the way you prepare today will change over time because of family dynamics, your increasing age, demographic and governmental changes. We need to constantly be on our toes and ready to pivot at a moment's

notice, a well thought out bug out plan that works today might not be your best option 5 or 10 years from now.

Here is a list of 10 personal doomsday scenarios that could affect the way you prep today or the way you prepare in the future. Scenarios like these are why I believe that where you should start preparing for your future begins with your financial and physical situation.

Loss of a Family Member

A loss of a family member could drastically affect not only how you prepare, but what you are able to prepare for. Losing the income of a family member could put you in a situation where you do not have the ability to purchase the supplies you need for any disaster you might face.

The loss of a family member could be because of divorce, death or even children moving away from home. Although a child moving out almost always helps your financial situation (it did for me) sometimes this is not the case, sometimes they are actually adding income to the family...I am not that fortunate.

Addition to the Family

Hopefully this is not a personal doomsday scenario for you, but I put it on this list because it will affect how you prepare and what your options are in the future. An infant will require more care and require you to prep differently than people without small children. Bugging out with a small child or elderly family member will also require you to acquire different supplies.

Local Grid Down Scenarios

Not only should we be concerned about larger off the grid events caused by an EMP or overpopulation and over usage, we should take into account the possibility of a local grid down situation that could affect us for weeks.

Disability

Accidents happen and life happens. A disability could mean you becoming disabled or a family member becoming disabled. There will be extra costs and medical expenses when caring for someone who has become disabled or different strategies needed when you are working on your bug out plan.

Auto Accident

An automobile accident could cause a number of different personal doomsday scenarios from finances to loss of a family member. A car accident could change your life in a split second. Even something as simple as your car breaking down could put your job in jeopardy.

Loss of Employment - Debt

Losing a job not only puts added stress on you and your family it handcuffs you and your ability to prep. Most Americans are only a few months away from a personal economic collapse at any given time.

Natural Disasters

Natural disasters can also cause other personal disasters to manifest. You could lose your home, your job and be completely cut off from the supplies you need in your daily life. Take a personal audit of what disasters are more likely in your area and make sure you are prepared for those before you even begin prepping for a larger scale disaster.

Loss of a Home

The loss of a home could be caused by many different factors. It could be caused by the loss of income and your home gets repossessed, a natural disaster could destroy your home or something caused inside the home like a fire or water lines breaking could make your home uninhabitable.

Robbery

Whether it is someone coming into your home and taking everything you own of someone stealing your car because you didn't lock it while you were just running into the store really quick to grab some lunch. Robbery could put a big financial strain on your prepping capabilities.

Mental Trauma - Physical Assault

This was brought up to me in the Facebook group by Heather and could present a huge problem not only for you, but your entire family as well. Many people who go through some sort of physical assault or situation that affects them mentally could be afraid to even leave their home.

Another member of the Facebook Group Steve commented...

"I think it is interesting what motivates one to prep in the first place. Why to some go to certain extremes but others are more practical? Is it a trauma? Is it upbringing?"

This is a very good point. There are many different reasons that cause someone to become a prepper, for me it was my upbringing, for others it is something that has caused them to open their eyes to the very real problems we face today.

Some people choose to be or become self-sufficient because they see the writing on the wall and they know that the current system is not sustainable, some have been raised their entire lives knowing a disaster could destroy the world as we know it and turn our lives upside down.

Ultimately the reason you are a prepper doesn't matter, just be thankful you are. God willing, we will live our whole lives and never have anything catastrophic happen to us, on the other hand by taking notice of current events and planning for an uncertain future we not only increase our chances for surviving an economic collapse, EMP or martial law, we make those smaller doomsday scenarios a little bit easier to handle.

What is the reason for your prepping? Was it just the way you were raised? Was it something that gradually turned the lights on? And one day you realized that most of the websites you visit are prepper websites. Or is there something that made you say "ok, this situation is more real than I ever imagined?

Chapter 4 - What Is a Prepper

"Some people see the glass half full. Others see it half empty. I see a glass

that's twice as big as it needs to be."

George Carlin

Before we get into what a "prepper" actually is we need to know how they talk. Some people hate these acronyms and some people use these acronyms all the time, regardless of where you stand the more you read, the more you will see these. And whether you use them or not you're going to need to know them.

Now I'm not going to go through every acronym and term you will hear because this video would take an hour to watch, but I am going to go over some of the terms you are most likely to hear as you begin to educate yourself about preparedness.

I also have a PDF that you can download that has a complete list on the resources page. But keep in mind, I did my best putting together this list, and I'm sure there are more out there, and I'm sure there are even some that I haven't heard of.

So let's dive into this list so hopefully when you are reading an article you don't have to stop and look up what TEOTWAWKI.

TEOTWAWKI is an acronym for the end of the world as we know it. This doesn't necessarily mean doomsday or Armageddon it's something that would not kill us, but change the way we need to live our lives. For kids TEOTWAWKI could be losing their cell phones, this could be the same for some adults although when I think of TEOTWAWKI I think of having to survive without power, water and heat.

TEOTWAWKI is synonymous with SHTF (Sh*t Hits the Fan) or WTSHTF (When the Sh*t Hits the Fan) and if you don't prepare you might need to GOOD – (Get out Of Dodge) or you could be SOL – Sh*t out of luck.

A few others will see are BOB, BIB, BOV and BOL these all involve Bugging Out.

You have a BOB which is a bug out bag

You have a BIB which is a bug in bag

You have a BOV which is a bug out vehicle

And a BOL which is a bug out location.

Why would you need to bug out? Good question. If you live in an urban area you are more likely to be surrounded by the GOLDEN HOARD which is basically swarms of people that are flipping out and want what you have and coming towards a town near you. The GOLDEN HORDE is made up of the POLLYANNA or SHEEPLE, these people blindly follow the masses and are in denial about world events

Or it could be because of an economic collapse that causes FIAT CURRENCY to become worthless and you need to own some JUNK SILVER (1964 or earlier silver coins)

 An EMP (electromagnetic pulse) could also cause an economic collapse because it would cause a GDE (Grid Down Event) or an OTGE (Off the Grid Event) An EMP could be caused by a CME (Coronal Mass Ejection) from the sun or a Carrington Event (caused by a large Coronal Mass Ejection) or even a HEMP (High Altitude Electromagnetic Pulse)

But don't worry, if you have a Faraday Cage (Used to shield electronics from an EMP) your iPad will still work...although the internet will probably be down.

All of this could cause our government to enact Martial Law because WROL (Without Rule of Law) the GOLDEN HORDE and the POLLYANNA'S would be after our LONG TERM FOOD STORAGE and we don't want to be in their LOS (Line of Sight)

You don't want to bug out with just the cloths on your back and it's SOP (Standard Operating Procedure) to have BOB or a 72 hour bag ready to go. You might use an ALICE backpack as your BOB which can also come with an ALICE frame. ALICE packs were created by the military To Reduce the load of the Infantry Combat Soldier and distribute weight more evenly.

The ALICE pack has been superseded by the MOLLE system meaning Modular Lightweight Load-carrying Equipment by the armed forces and some preppers as well.

The MOLLE system is modular because of the use of the PALS (Pouch Attachment Ladder System) and allows you to add storage space. You might not want to use an ALICE frame for your BIB because a bug in bag is for getting from where you are to your BIL (bug in location) these could be stored in your car or taken with you when you leave home. I personally choose the MOLLE system but the choice is yours. Price might play a role in this as well.

Along with medical supplies, water, weapons and survival gear you might want to have some MRE's (meals Ready To Eat) or some C-Ration (Combat ration) to eat along the way, but try to avoid food from Monsanto because it is made from GMO (Genetically Modified Organisms)

So, FWIW: (For What It's Worth) if the SHTF because of an EMP or an OTGE Well basically YOYO (You're On Your Own) and you won't be able to depend on FEMA (Federal Emergency Management System) or ARC (American Red Cross) for your safety. You need to take your survival in your own hands and have a BOB or an INCH (I'm Never Coming Home Kit) that you can put in your BOV to get to your BOL or Isolated Retreat (A BOL but better) It might be a good idea to get a HAM RADIO license or have a crank radio JIC (Just in Case) you have no other way of communicating with the people around you.

And if were in a GDE you might want to have some FIAT CURRENCY or some JUNK SILVER because you won't be able to get money from the ATM (automated Teller Machine) and you might not have the money in your account that you thought you had.

Long list right, honestly this probably doesn't even cover all of the terms and acronyms you will hear, but it gives you a good idea and a good starting point so you don't have to google every term and acronym you come across while you're reading articles and learning about preparedness.

So what is a prepper?

When you ask someone their definition of a "Prepper" most people will tell you a prepper is someone who is paranoid, crazy or an extremist. Storing food, water, fuel and supplies do not make us crazy or paranoid like most people think, as a matter of fact it makes you responsible. There really isn't one definition you can use to define a prepper.

We all have different reason, different circumstances and many other defining factors that go into why we prep to be able to put all preppers into one category. This is like saying everyone from the Middle East is a terrorist. How can we label everyone from the Middle East a terrorist if all we see about them is from the news channels?

Think about it, everyone in the world has an opinion about what Americans are like, but we know very well that the picture these people have of Americans was painted by what our government does and not who we are as people.

Unfortunately this is exactly why we are labeled as paranoid alarmists, when people see something on TV it becomes reality to them without questioning the source, and without giving it a second thought.

We need to make sure we don't fall into this same trap, this includes the prepping and survivalist blogs we read. Everyone has their own agenda and own reasons for putting out the information they do, and it's up to us to dig a little deeper when something interests us and not just read one article and call it fact. My rule of thumb is that if I can't find at least three different sources stating the same facts I am hesitant as to its validity.

You can take the term prepper and break it down into 5 categories. You can take each of these categories and break them down further but for now let's start with these.

The Extreme Prepper

For the most part this is how the mainstream media like to portray us, and therefore how we are perceived by most people. Shows like doomsday preppers only help to perpetuate this stereotype because they like to highlight extreme preppers like these on their show for rating and viewers.

Let's face it, the everyday prepper is just not sexy enough to make a show about, you and I might watch, but it is far too boring and wouldn't fit into the average Americans lifestyle.

An extreme prepper will literally go off the deep end prepping for one disaster, and not just a natural disaster, they prepare for a large scale disaster like an EMP, Bio Terror or a pandemic. Although all of these are real threats we face, an extreme prepper will basically forget about all the other disaster scenarios and focus on one. The media loves these guys, and my feeling is that these guys love the media too.

The Open Minded Prepper

If people decide to do a little research on what prepping and the preparedness lifestyle actually is they begin to find out that the majority of preppers fall into this category. Someone who is open minded sees the bigger picture and knows that it doesn't make sense to install a home security system when the house is on fire.

This is the category Lisa and I fall into, it just doesn't make sense to focus all of your energy on one scenario just to get blindsided by something you never saw coming because you were too busy building an underground bunker.

I'm not saying an underground bunker isn't a good idea, I'm just saying take a look at the bigger picture and plan accordingly.

The Gateway Prepper

This is probably where most of us start. Something or someone has peaked our interest in preparedness and self-sufficiency and before we know it we are one of those crazy preppers.

What gets one into prepping is different for all of us, it could be a personal doomsday like a job loss or death in the family, or it could be the fact that you just can't ignore what is going on in the world today and want to know what you can do about it.

What you begin to find out is that there is nothing you can do about the economy or a terrorist attack, but you can take some precautions that will better your odds in the long run. Like they say, a good offense is the best defense, and being prepared and knowing how to be self-sufficient during trying times increases your odds of survival.

If you fall into this category, welcome aboard, you will be an open minded crazy prepper like the rest of us in no time.

The Survivalist

Survivalists and preppers often get lumped into the same category, this is because there are so many things that survivalists and preppers do that intersect with each other. At its core both groups have one goal, to be prepared and skilled enough to survive if the SHTF in some way or another.

The survivalist is someone who is or has learned to live off the land or off the grid, someone who fully expects to bug out rather than bug in. Again, there are many different types of survivalists so you can't label all survivalists as mountain men (or women)

I named my website Survivalist Prepper because I am interested in both. Although I do love the outdoors and learning new skills that could become useful in the future, I am not so naive to think that surviving for years in the mountains would be a cake walk, but I like to think I could do fairly well.

I am more of a survivalist and Lisa is more of a prepper, but we are both concerned about the same things, self-sufficiency and what we would do if and when the inevitable happens. It never hurts to learn about everything you can because you never know when you are going to use it.

The Closet Prepper

The closet prepper would be someone who just isn't ready to tell anyone about their fears. This could be because of their career or family or they are too afraid of opening up because they don't want to be labeled "off their rocker" or be told " oh! Your one of those crazy prepper type people" Kind of like when someone believes in God but is too concerned about being ridiculed to say anything about it.

There are many different reason why someone would be hesitant to talk about their interest in preparing and their concern about our current society, but wouldn't it be nice if the S did HTF and the neighbor that you thought was one of the sheeple pulled out his bug out bag and shotgun and said "let's get to work"

Generally Speaking

As I said not all preppers are created equal, regardless of what the mainstream media would like you to believe. Preppers by nature are quiet about what they do, and for good reason, you don't want to jeopardize everything you have done by telling the world how much food, water and ammunition you have stored, by doing this you make yourself a bigger target than the guy next door with nothing.

Just like religion and nationality you can't say that just because someone believes in God they are Christian, and just because someone lives in Ireland they drink a lot, these are unfair generalizations that do not reflect the differences that make us all human.

Regardless of why you prep or how long you have been doing it the only thing that matters is that you are. These people that give you a hard time or label you a nut are going to be looking to you when the SHTF, and it's up to you at that point whether you help them out or send them off and say "who's crazy now?."

What Are You Prepping For

Anyone who considers themselves a prepper or survivalist should know what you are prepping for. Every survival situation requires a different approach and strategy to ensure you have the best possible chance to defend yourself and your family. Your plan should give you the best possible chance to

1. Defend your family

2. Defend everything that you have stockpiled while preparing for your survival.

Being prepared is just the first step we need to take to increase the odds of our survival if everything hits the fan. Understanding that we are the minority and that 99% of the U.S. population will be caught with their pants down is the second step. These people could be your next door neighbor, your pastor of family doctor. Desperate times has a way of changing even the most pure and good hearted person into a person that will do whatever it takes to survive. As preppers this makes us huge targets because we have what these people failed to prepare for and now need.

What you are prepping for depends on your situation and what you will need to do in that environment to survive. Like I said everyone that is unprepared will be after you and your cache,water and food could become more valuable than gold. The first thing you need to think about is how are you going to protect everything you have stockpiled preparing for this situation? And how do your surroundings dictate what you will need to do?

How you decide to prepare all depends on where you live and your surroundings. If you live in a big city you will need to have a completely different strategy for protecting yourself that if you live in a rural area. Either way one thing is certain, anyone who is unprepared will be looking to take advantage of your foresight and knowledge.

Prepping In an Urban Setting

There are a couple of different strategies I think you have if you live in the city, one is to bug out and the other is to stay your ground. Both will have their challenges and really depend on your awareness about all of the possible scenarios and what give you the best chance for survival.

1. Bugging Out: Keep in mind that as you try to bug out that you will not be alone, you will probably find that everyone that is unprepared will want to be your new best friend, you should probably find a way to break away from everyone and everything that you can. This could mean taking the toughest path and finding out where everyone is going and go the other way. Inevitably you will run into someone who has become desperate and will do whatever it takes to survive and they will be thinking *"I just found my new best friend"* and you should be thinking *"one more step and I'm dropping this sucker"* You've probably heard this before but TRUST NO ONE!

This is where having your bug out bag and being prepared for situations like these are crucial. A bug out bag should not only have supplies such as food, water, first aid and clothing it should contain items for personal protection for you and your family. I wrote a series of 3 articles about what I carry in my bug out bag as well as my family's bug out bags. If you have time have a look at them at www.survivalistprepper.net. They are very detailed and might give you some ideas.

2. Bugging In: Staying put and fortifying your position is another option, although by doing this you better be prepared to defend yourself from the start. I think the biggest challenge of this strategy is going to be right after everything hits the fan. And even if you plan on staying your ground you should still have a plan in place to move quickly if the situation arises. When the chaos is at it's peak and everyone is looting and flipping out is when you will be the most vulnerable. As people begin to leave town and try to find a safer place to be it could turn out to be less of a full on assault...but don't let your guard down, there will always be someone who wants something from you.

This is just my opinion but if I was in this situation I think I would wait out the storm and try to "sneak out" after the first wave of the hysterical flipped out crazy's left town. I just wouldn't feel safe staying in one spot during the beginning stages of some kind of economic or governmental meltdown.

Prepping In a Rural Setting

Some of the basic prepping principals apply to both urban and rural survival, there are some differences you will need to take into account though. One of these is knowing that in the beginning stages of any meltdown you will have a little (very little) buffer before everyone fleeing the city's make it out to you. Another advantage that a rural setting has it that you usually have more property to work with and if you own that property you have more ability to prepare as opposed to living in an apartment or rented home. I don't think most landlords would be willing to let you build a survival bunker in the back yard.

1. Bugging In: Defending your property really depends on where you live and how far away from the major population you live. Take me for example, I live about 40 miles outside of Denver on 10 acres of land, this has its pluses and minuses. On the plus side I own my home and have plenty of land to build an underground bunker (which I plan on doing soon) and construct it in a way that it will be hidden so the looters and opportunists will not be able to find me or my family...and if they do I will make sure they wish they had never found it. On the down side 40 miles is not that far at all, on top of that I live about the same distance away from Colorado Springs which is an Air Force town. So to say the least I don't feel like I have the perfect position to fortify and in that situation the military would present a bigger threat that a crazed starving business man with his Swiss Army Knife and a ski pole.

2. Bugging Out: As I said before you should always have a plan to bug out. Unless you live deep in the woods and on top of a mountain you should be prepared for any situation. Not all of us are woodsman and have the opportunity to live this lifestyle, we only get to practice while we continue our daily routines so we can continue to support our family. This doesn't mean we should throw in the towel though, we just have a little bigger challenge ahead of us. You need to assess your situation and decide what the best plan of action is for different scenarios.

So What Are You Prepping For?

What you are prepping for all depends on your personal situation and surroundings. Being a good prepper does not mean having the most expensive survival knife or hand gun. These can all be taken away from you in a second if you are not aware of your surroundings and prepared to fight for what is yours. Thinking about all the different possible scenarios and having contingency plans in place are crucial to your survival. So whether you live in the city or in the suburbs you need to be aware of your surroundings, plan for the worst and hope for the best.

Chapter 5 – Building the Foundation

"By failing to prepare, you are preparing to fail."

Benjamin Franklin

Start With the Right Mindset

Regardless of your situation everything starts in that melon sitting on your head. If you don't have the right mindset you could very likely find yourself less prepared than you thought you were. Prepping shouldn't start with stockpiling a bunch of beans and rice, it starts with you taking an honest look at your situation and fixing it. The things you do in your daily life that could hinder your ability to survive any sort of chaotic situation.

How you prep and what you prep really depends on your situation. If you live in an urban area, or an apartment you might not have the room store 100 gallons of water so you might be better served preparing to bug out. If you live in a suburban or rural area you might want to work on your homesteading skills.

If you are in debt up to your ears or have a limited income (like most of us) you might want to take a hard look at what you need and what you don't need, and what you can spend money on that could serve you better elsewhere.

Unfortunately preppers have this stigma of being alarmists who have their houses filled with MRE's and Guns just waiting for the end of the world. As you know this is not the case. We just choose to look at the bigger picture, keep our eyes open and plan for our own safety and survival without any government assistance. Preppers and survivalist are not all about doom and gloom, we should all be working towards being responsible self-sufficient adults.

I have recently listened to a couple of episodes of the Survival Podcast with Jack Spirko called "Holy crap, I just found out everything isn't super" (2 part series) and I have to say, if you have never listened to Jack you should at least check those episodes out, he offers some great advice about how you should look at prepping as a lifestyle and not just preparing for the end of the world.

Jack goes into detail in the podcast about how and where to start you're prepping but one thing that stood out to me, and I feel is overlooked is the prepper mindset. You can get all the information you want about how much water you need to store, how to purify it and what you need in a good bug out bag, but there is not that much information about how we should think as preppers.

Lower you're Debt

The first step you should take is figuring out what you do on a daily basis that puts you at risk. This could be anything from eating at McDonald's everyday which affects your health and your wallet to how financially stable you are.

If you are $50,000 dollars in debt, you might want to solve that problem before you go out and spend thousands of dollars on solar panels, generators and bug out supplies. Getting out of debt is not only necessary, it is our responsibility. As he says in the podcast, you can't blame your momma and you can't blame Obama, you dug this hole yourself and you need to get yourself out of it.

If we continually buy everything on credit we are not getting out of this imaginary money market that we all know will inevitably collapse. In turn, that problem becomes our problem. It honestly might take you 5 years to get out of debt, but once you are out of debt, you can invest in your future, whether that be gold, silver or solar panels and taking steps towards living off the grid.

Investments

When you say investment people automatically think stocks, bonds and 401k's. As a prepper we need to think the opposite, get away from the paper assets and move towards investing in your future. Someone who has 50K in a retirement plan could have all of that wiped out in no time at all. But someone who has invested in gold and silver will still have that when and if the economy goes to crap. If you can't hold it in your hand, it's not real.

All investments are not just monetary, if you spend $600 on a generator, home fortifications or even 20 gas cans to store fuel, these are investments. Think of everything you do as an investment in your future, if you cannot honestly label it an investment you should ask yourself "can I live without this?"

Ask Yourself What If?

Always ask yourself what if? This is why we prepare; we are basically our own insurance policy. We need to take our personal situation and ask ourselves "what poses the biggest threat to me and my family right now?" and "what if this happens?" We need to always keep our eyes open and our ears peeled because even the smallest inconceivable situation could turn bad in a second.

If someone knows you take the same route to work every day and always stop by the bank on your way home, you are a target. If you go to a gas station and leave your keys in the ignition, you are a target. Even if you live in a rural area like me you still have to think what if?

My kids are terrible about locking the door behind them as they go to school because they think "we live in the boonies; no one is going to break in." This drives me bonkers! And the fact is, it could happen anywhere at any time.

Something as simple as locking a door or taking your keys out of the ignition takes 5 seconds, and could save you hundreds of dollars, undue stress and even save your life.

Prep with a Plan

As I was skimming across some of the many e-mails I get in regard to prepping, and I came across one that caught my interest. I came across The Patriot Nurse She has a couple of links to YouTube videos and in one she was talking with a student of one of her classes who happens to be a long distance truck driver. He works for a trucking company, because it is too expensive for him to work for himself.

And this is where I got interested. He talked about how he can tell how the economy is by the number of truckers on the roads. He said that he has been a truck driver since 1999, and up until 2004, when he would pull into truck stops, if he got in too late all of the spaces for overnight parking were full. However he started noticing a general decline in the number of trucks at each truck stop that would park overnight. He also said it hasn't gotten any better. Fair estimate would be 50 to 60% less trucks on the roads. That means fewer trucks making deliveries to grocery stores. Which if you think about it is a little frightening.

It's always good to have food storage and a plan in place if a natural disaster, economic collapse or EMP were to affect your life, but as preppers we need to look at the big picture and take steps towards becoming self-sufficient.

How this all plays out really depends on your personal situation and what steps you need to take before you fill your house with 1000lbs of beans and install solar panels, if your house gets foreclosed on or you have to move, these mean nothing.

Start from the inside out, make a list for yourself and layout the path that is the most plausible and will allow you to reach your goals.

And remember, it doesn't have to all be done overnight, prepping is a lifestyle and you will never really be fully prepared for anything, and fully Prepared to bug out if that becomes necessary.

How Did They Ever Survive 100 Years Ago?

As a society we are only concerned by what is affecting us right now. We don't worry about water until it's gone or undrinkable. We don't worry about our money disappearing from the bank because that just never happens, and yes it does. We don't prepare for an earthquake or natural disaster until our home is destroyed. And worst of all we as a society we have this unfounded faith that our government has our best interests in mind, and will be there to bail us out when the SHTF. I'm not saying we need to live completely off the grid, but we need to know how, if and when that time comes.

Everything is so easy today. You need food, you run out to the grocery store and get it. You need a new shirt? You run out to your local store and get it. Right now, anything you want you can get either by going to the store or buying it online. But what would you do if you couldn't get to the store, or the thing you wanted wasn't there? Most American's don't believe that could happen. Actually, most American's probably have never even thought about it.

Our society today teaches us to choose the easier path, why work harder when you can work smarter. An unfortunately our society is paying the price. Everywhere you look, if you have your eyes open the signs are becoming more and more prevalent that something is seriously wrong with this once great nation of ours. Our corrupt government tells us everything is ok. The mass media feeds their versions of the news for millions of American's. And the saddest part about it is they don't think anything is wrong!

Thankfully, you have realized things aren't quite right in our nation, and you may or may not be wondering what do you do about it? What do you need to do first? The most important thing you need to do is learn. There are many websites and many articles that you will find that can help you in your quest for knowledge. Read books, listen to podcasts, and learn from the experts. The more you know, the better prepared you will be for different situations. The steps you need to take for yourself and your family will be different than the steps I have taken for my family. But maybe reading what someone else has done to get prepared might get your own ideas going.

Tips for the Beginning Prepper

When I began my journey of becoming a "prepper" (I prefer the term self-reliant though) I didn't want to tell anyone. I knew my friends and family would think I was crazy, and finally went off the deep end. So unfortunately a lot of the planning and research I did was alone. So here are some tips to get you started in the right direction.

Create lists: Start making lists of everything you want to learn, and everything you think you will need. You can customize the lists later on, but having a starting point helps to get your thoughts down on paper.

Find alternative news sources: The mass media is owned by the corporations that want you to hear only their version of what is newsworthy. Question everything you hear on the 'news' because most of it is keeping your attention from the real news. There are many different places you can find what is really happening. But trust what you know, and even though it is hard, don't get caught up in everything you see on the news.

Question everything: Whether it is the mainstream news or a website that peaks your interest, keep an open mind. There are just as many prepper news websites with their own agendas out there as there are mass media channels spreading propaganda, the only difference is the money available to them.

Start living with less: this is not easy at first, but it gets easier. Pay off your debt, and live within your means. Even better, live well below your means, and keep doing it. I mean, do you really need 150 channels to watch? Do you really need that new car? Do you really need that designer bag? You already know the answer to these things. That's the easy part. The hard part is actually doing it. You can do it, start small and build on it. Stop eating out, and spend more time with your family. For the same cost of a meal out, you can probably eat at least three meals at home. And starting small like this isn't that difficult. One bonus of this is by eating more at home, you will find when you do have a special occasion and choose to go out, it doesn't taste as good for some reason. Bu the bigger bonus is you will be spending time with your family, and that is worth a lot more than money.

Learn how to garden: This sounds easy doesn't it? Well, it can be, and it can be really difficult. But the only way you are going to learn is by doing it. Start learning about your dirt, mark off an area, or try a container garden or raised bed garden. My favorite book on gardening is [Mini Farming Self-Sufficiency on ¼ Acre] It is 20 chapters of very practical and useable information. Even if you don't have a ¼ acre, you can apply the same principles, just on a smaller scale to the area you can garden in.

Get in shape: And I don't mean by going to the gym, but if that is what works best for you, do it. Get off of your couch, shut off the TV, and go do something. Go for a hike, go play in your yard, go play with your kids. All of the advice of getting thirty minutes of exercises a day is a good piece of advice, but you don't have to do it without doing something productive in return. Being more self-reliant will do a lot for your physical fitness. You don't need to go to a gym to work on those flabby upper arms, get out and dig some dirt, or pull some weeds. Not only will you save money on a gym membership, but your yard will look great! And the hard work you do on a daily basis will get you more prepared for how to take care of your family.

Have alternative methods of cooking and heating: This can be as simple as using your wood burning fireplace, or having a wood burning stove (you should probably know how to collect fire wood, too.) How did anyone survive 100 years ago? We better pay attention to history, learn from it, and be prepared to live without microwaves.

Food Storage: There are thousands of articles and books on this topic. Do your research, and do what is right for you and your family, don't follow someone else's list unless it's right for you. But that's an easy fix, find a list and make your own. Start small, add a few extra cans of food to your weekly grocery store trip. You will be surprised at how much food you can accumulate in about three months with spending maybe twenty extra dollars a week.

Build a library: all of those articles and e-books you have been reading, print them out and put them in a binder. If it's a great article, save it so you will have it for later, and you can always go back and re-read it later on.

Getting Back To the Basics

Learning from history will help build your knowledge and prepare you for what can and will happen in the future. As you begin prepping this list will keep growing, there are many other important things to consider while prepping and stockpiling. This is how I got started, and what I did in the beginning of becoming more prepared, and self-reliant. Hopefully this will give you some areas to start working on, and you can build your own list, and your skills. Welcome to the club!

How to Be Properly Prepared?

Being prepared is something that every single American really needs to be doing. There are approximately three hundred sixteen million people living in the United States today, and according to Google, about three million Americans consider themselves to be preppers. This probably doesn't include those who have never visited any preppers websites, and those who just have continued to live that way, because that is all they know. However, with an increasing number of Americans finally catching on to the fact that something isn't quite right in this once great nation of ours.

We thought it would be equally important to think about some of the areas of prepping that people can make mistakes with. I myself have been guilty of more than one item on this list, how about you? Take a look at our list, and see how you measure up.

1. False sense of security

With so much in the news today about guns, gun regulation, and new laws aimed at disarming us, more people than ever are buying guns, ammunition and the like. But just because you have a gun, do you know how to use it? Have you trained how to use it? And if you have, are you prepared to use it on another human being? It's one thing to think you can, but it is a completely different thing to be staring into the eyes of another person and really know yes, you are prepared to take their life. Just because you have a gun, or any other weapon, does not mean you are secure or safe. You need to have the training, and experience to go along with it.

And it isn't just related to guns and security. You have food, ok a lot of food. But how long will that food really last? Have you thought about that? And what happens when the food runs out? What will you do? These are things you need to think about, and have a plan for. That is what prepping is all about, being prepared, but it is also about knowing your limitations. If something can go wrong it usually will. Keep that in mind when you are prepping.

2. Not being prepared for the right situations

Unfortunately reality T.V. has pointed this out. Finding people that are planning for such catastrophic events as a complete reversal of the North and South Pole, and those who are planning for a huge asteroid to land in the Pacific Ocean, or the Madrid Fault opening up. Now don't get me wrong, those are all possible events that could happen. However, there are many other more regional situations that take place every single day that require people to be prepared. If you live in an area prone to flooding, then that is something you should seriously be preparing for. The same goes for tornadoes, and hurricanes. In our area, devastating wild fires passed uncomfortably close to our home. So for our family, planning for an EMP is not at the top of my list, but protecting my home against wild fires is. Know your area and the potential situations that you will find yourself in, and plan for it. You can always plan for the zombie apocalypse, but it would be to your advantage to prepare for what happens in your own backyard.

I have to add that being prepared for the situations that can happen in your area also means knowing when to leave. You have that bug out bag for a reason. Yes you will be leaving your home, but you need to weight the risks if you stay. If you leave, your home may be looted. (So this would be a good time to make sure your supplies that you are leaving are well hidden.) But if you stay, you and your family may die. And never wait until the last minute when an evacuation order happens in your area. If it walks like a duck...I think you know where this is going. Do not let your pride or your lack of trust in the authorities cost you or your family their lives.

3. Not looking at the bigger picture

This is one area that I have been guilty of ignoring. When you begin prepping and planning, it can be easy to lose sight of the bigger picture of why you are doing this. True, you want to be self-sustaining and be able to provide for your family. But then what? When the economy does collapse, and you are safe in your home with your family, do you think about the other three hundred million people that may or may not be outside of your door? Pretending the rest of the world has disappeared while you have been preparing isn't the case. You will run out of food, and you will run out of ammunition. You will not be able to fight everyone off. So even though you will be able to hold out for a good long time, eventually you will have to think about educating the masses to what you have learned, and how they too can be self-reliant. Remember you can feed a man a meal, or teach him to fish so he can feed himself.

4. Lack of networks

I can't speak for anyone other than myself on this matter, but from the way the mass media has portrayed preppers, I don't run around my neighborhood and make sure everyone knows I am a prepper. I prefer to keep this to myself. But I need to stop that way of thinking, just as you do, and it isn't easy. I am always paying attention to others, and watching what they do. I have "come out" to several people, and I was shocked to learn that they are preppers too. I can honestly say it felt as if a wave of relief had washed over me when I realized I wasn't alone. And too see the expression on their faces, they were grateful to know they weren't alone either. So I challenge you to put yourself out there a little bit. Keep your cautious hat on, but test the waters, and you may find out that your neighbor, or co-worker or best friends Aunt Mary is a prepper too.

5. Not having the skills necessary to sustainability

Just because you have enough food to feed a family of six for two years does not mean you are sustainable. Like I said earlier, that food will run out, and then what? Do you have a plan in place to sustain your family and your way of life? You need to know how to continue once your initial stores have been depleted. You need to know how to grow a garden, kill a chicken, could you survive off of food found in the wilderness and defend yourself and your home? If you have an injury, you will need to know how to take care of it. Do you know what to do to treat an open wound to get it to heal so you don't end up with a life threatening infection? These are things you need to know how to deal with, because things like this will happen.

6. Lack of education

Just because you have it, doesn't mean you know how to use it. Take the time now to learn everything you can about survival, economics, how to 'read' people, and everything you can get your hands on. And if you find more information that you just can't absorb now, print it out and save it for later. You will never know everything, and you will always have the capability of learning. Knowledge is free, and it doesn't weigh anything to carry it around in your brain.

7. Stockpiling the wrong items

This can happen believe it or not, and it often does. If your family has never eaten SPAM before, a stressful life changing environment is not a good time to suddenly throw it at them. Store what you eat, and eat what you store. Introduce fresh vegetables to your family now. Start trying new recipes now that incorporate what you will plan on storing. If you are going to be growing pinto beans as a main carbohydrate, introduce them in meals now. You may find you don't even like pinto beans. So that means finding something that you can like, and has lots of options. Because if you have three years' worth of MRE's to eat, and then you discover no one in your family can tolerate them life is going to get really hard really fast.

8. Storing all of your preps in the same place

You have worked way too hard for all of your supplies and preps to be lost in a single event. Do your research. In the event of a fire, flood, or other disaster, if you kept everything in one place, the chances are pretty high that with just one disaster, all of your stuff is going to be wiped out. And then where would you be? You got it, just like about 90% of the United States population, unprepared and out of luck.

Now granted, by having a network of likeminded friends, and cohorts, even if this did happen, you would have a network of people around you to help. But I don't want others to have to provide for me, when I could have done it for myself in the first place by thinking ahead.

Always store caches in different areas. Whether it's a storage unit close by, some in your home, and some outside of your home, the garage, the barn, the dog house. Where ever, keep your supplies split up because you need to plan that something will inevitably happen to part of your storage plan.

9. Getting Too Comfortable

I should again raise my hand on this one. We all do it. It is too easy not to in today's society. Everything around us screams comfort, and that's what we all want, isn't it? I wrote an article about how the money we have in banks could put a major kink in our lives because we depend on them. Even though it isn't easy, you have to break away from the comfort. You have to get up and go to work every day, and then come home every day, and work just as hard at making sure your garden is growing, and that your rain water collection system is working. Every day will present new challenges for you, and every day you will have to push forward and forgo the comfort of your couch. So get up and do it. Don't put off until tomorrow what you should be doing today.

10. Losing focus

This is a nice way of saying stop being lazy! Do not procrastinate. There is no time for this. The only one who will judge you on this is yourself. There is no passing grade, no ribbon. But if you stay focused, and have a plan it will be difficult not to be successful. A good way to do this is write everything down. Get a couple of spiral bound notebooks, and start making lists. List out what you need to learn. List out your budget for supplies. List out the luxuries you would really want to have in your stores, and figure out a way to make it happen. You are only limited by yourself. Don't let negativity get in the way of your goals.

This by no means is an all-inclusive list, these are just the things I have paid attention too, and areas that tend to cause problems for preppers.

There are so many websites sharing lots of different information and I urge you to check them out as you can. You will find you can never know enough when it comes to being prepared.

Now that we have some of the basics down and some of the dos and don'ts, let's dig a little deeper in and take a look at some ways to become more prepared and self-sufficient. Let's start at the very beginning and work our way up to becoming a seasoned prepper.

Taking a Personal Audit

As I said earlier prepping doesn't start with building an underground bunker, prepping begins in your own home and in your own pocket book. If you are not prepared to pay your rent or your mortgage you have no business trying to prepare for the end of the world, because the end of your world could come next month.

The first step to becoming more self-sufficient is getting your personal affairs in order. This does not mean you need to put off buying supplies and food storage until you are out of debt, it just means that you will be limited when it comes to how much you can afford until you get some of your bills paid down or figure out a way to make your financial situation a little better.

Let's talk about some of the ways you can earn some extra money to pay off debt or supplement your income to afford some of the supplies you need, and then we will get into taking a personal audit of your situation and formulate a plan that works best for you.

You might be thinking right now "what is this freak talking about?" And I don't blame you. Don't let a blue duck take you out sounds like some crazy passage from the paramilitary version of a Dr. Seuss book, and I'm questioning my sanity as I write this. But stick with me for a minute and this should all make sense...I hope.

Don't Let a Blue Duck Take You Out

You might be saying to yourself "There is no such thing as a blue duck!" and you are right, in the physical sense. The fact that we would never expect to see a blue duck is exactly what makes it possible.

Some people call these black swan events, I choose to call these blue duck events because it's more memorable and well, I'm a little weird sometimes.

We all have differing opinions on some of the events below, but for the sake of this article we a going on the assumption that they all happened the way we have been told they did.

Events like the rise of Hitler, the stock market crash of 1929, the attack on Pearl Harbor, Sandy Hook, Columbine High School and even 9-11 are all events that were completely unexpected and changed history. If people had paid more attention most of these events could have been avoided.

The psychological biases that make people individually and collectively blind to uncertainty and unaware of the massive role of a rare event is exactly what makes these blue duck events, or "black swan", if you're not weird like me, possible.

These hard to predict, rare events that are beyond the realm of normal expectations in history, science, finance, and technology have the potential to be life changing on a personal scale, to history changing on a global scale.

We spend so much time concentrating on food storage, supplies and living without modern convinces we forget that regardless of how much we prepare and how "ready" we think we are something always come up that takes us by surprise.

We are preparing for some of these events, and for the most part this is exactly why we prepare. We want to be ready for any kind of natural disaster, we want to be prepared for any event that takes us off the grid and we want to be prepared for when our own government decides that we have done such a great job preparing that we need to share with the less fortunate...that's a whole different article!

"True stability results when presumed order and presumed disorder are balanced. A truly stable system expects the unexpected and is prepared to be disrupted and waits to be transformed."

Tim Robbins

What If?

The question I ask myself all the time is "By focusing all of my attention on all of this other stuff am I setting myself up to get blindsided?" Here are a few things that crossed my mind...

Insufficient Funds

What if I went to the bank to withdraw some money and I got the dreaded "insufficient funds" notice? Do I have enough cash on hand and precious metals to withstand this? And how comfortable am I with the amount of money I have in the bank and what would I do if it all disappeared? Because it could...

Accidents

What if someone in my family got into a car accident? Would they know what to do? How would I react if it was something serious? And how would this affect me now and in the future?

I don't even like to think about this, but if we want to take a realistic look at our situation death and unforeseen accidents should be part of your thought process, especially in a SHTF scenario.

Mind & Body

How healthy are my family and I really? We sometimes take this for granted because we can go on for years without anything too bad happening to us, but one day unexpectedly this could change causing a whole different set of problems in the future.

Sadly, this is something that never crossed my mind 20 years ago and now it seems to cross my mind daily. You gotta love getting old.

All in the Family

I'm pretty confident in my abilities, but what about my family? Would my children know how to get home if something happened? This is a tricky situation sometimes because the typical teenager has different concerns than we do, basically everything is a blue duck to them and they just roll with the punches.

I think this is something that is sometimes over looked and something we seriously need to consider. The reason most of us do this is to protect our family and without them everything else becomes irrelevant.

Can I live Off the Grid...Really?

As I just said, I am pretty confident in my abilities but could I really grow enough food to sustain my family if I had to? Do I have the right resources in place for energy, water, shelter and self-defense? Self-sufficiency and living off the grid is going to be harder than we give it credit for, and there is no such thing as being completely self-sufficient.

Missed it by That Much

Another question I asked myself is how many "projects" I have that are half done? One glaring project is a well pump. I have a huge resource of water sitting right below me but if the power goes out I have no way of getting to it.

We have been talking about getting a hand well pump for some time now but what if everything goes down the tubes tomorrow? The answer is simple, we would be hosed. I guess it's time to stop talking and start doing.

Make a list of unfinished projects so they don't get placed on the back burner and finish them...a well pump is on the top of my list.

Shock & Awe

How will catastrophic events affect not only me but my family as well? And how well will we handle those situations psychologically?

Because we have had the fortune to live in a time without much turmoil on our soil I'm not so sure that we are ready to handle it if enemy troops invaded or launched a missile at us, martial law was enacted or any event that causes mass casualties from biological elements to mother nature having a hissy fit.

I think that eventually we would overcome any situation like this but how will we react during the crisis? And will we be around after the crisis is the question.

The Dangers of Complacency

By nature we become terribly complaisant as we go through our lives, we drive back and forth to work, we go to the ATM when we need a few dollars and we assume that we are going to wake up the next day and do the same thing over again.

All of these routines have become habit and we tend to get tunnel vision and don't see that guided missile coming right at us out of the corner of our eye.

Like I said earlier this is what we do, this is why we prepare. We don't want to get blindsided by some catastrophic event, and we want to be as ready as we can possibly be if something life changing does happen.

As prepared as we all "think" we are we need to take a realistic view of our situation and ask ourselves what if? And how many times have I justified not getting something done by saying "I'm doing pretty good" or "As soon as I get the time I am going to…"

As they say close only counts in horse shoes and hand grenades.

Chapter 6 - Funding Your Prepper Lifestyle

"A wise person should have money in their head, but not in their heart."

Jonathan Swift

Taking on the lifestyle of someone who is more prepared is an admiral trait, in my humble opinion. Unfortunately, getting started can and is, not only a daunting task, but it can be expensive as well. No matter how you look at it, prepping costs money. Even if you are really thrifty and creative with your money, supplies still cost money.

You can put a little bit away each month, and buy your supplies as you can, which is a smart way to do it. By spending a little each week or month, you will be amazed at the amount of food and supplies you can amass by purchasing a little bit at a time. You need to prioritize what you need to buy, and work your way through your list, one item at a time.

The first step is creating a list of what it is you want to achieve. It doesn't matter what you put on your list, it's *your* list. Start with categories, and then you can go from there. There are a few categories that you should consider listing, but remember this is your list, and you should lit the things that you need and want to have for your own preparations.

For example, these are categories that are important to me and my family:

1. Water

2. Food

3. Shelter

4. Outside Items

5. Inside Items

6. Tools

7. Land

And that's pretty much it (for now.) Like I said earlier, this is the way I categorized the things that my family and I will need, so if your list is different, that's great! Make it your own, but make the goal that you will create a list, and put everything down that you will need, or you would like to have.

It is a good thing for you to come up with what is important for you, because it is your list, and this will help you to be accountable for it. Because if someone tells you to make a list, and put the following items on it, it won't mean anything to you.

The best part of creating lists such as this is you get to cross things off as you get them. It is pretty powerful to be able to create a list, and 3 months later you have crossed off everything under one category. Keep your list handy, so you can always add to it, and make a point to review it, and continue to improve on it. Make it a part of your life, and make it a habit.

And even though this is fun, what happens next is even better...for some reason, when you create lists of items you want to have, you actually achieve these items. So start small, and work your way up. You will be able to do it.

But if your weekly income is going to pay all of the bills you have, there may not be a lot of money left over every month in order to start your preparing. If this is the case for you, it's time to start looking at all of the options that are available to you. And yes, you do have options.

1. A Second Job

This may not be the most attractive option, but it is an option. If you seriously want to become more prepared, and live a more self-reliant lifestyle, sometimes in order to achieve that you will need to suck it up, and get a second job.

A way to make this more appealing is to put a time limit on it. Say for example your goal is to have 6 months' worth of food, and to pay off your credit cards. Figure out what this would cost you, and divide that total by the amount of months you are willing to work that second job. Not only will you have a plan, but there will be a light at the end of the tunnel for how long you will need to work those extra hours.

2. A Home Based Business

Another option would be to start a home based business. This may sound like a daunting task, but it really isn't that hard. Think about it, everyone has a hobby. Now, if you can take that hobby and make some money with it, you may be able to bypass the second job, and spend that time working for yourself.

As an example, this is what I did with the help of my wife. By a complete accident, we ended up with a nice little side income that has allowed us to be able to increase our food storage, as well as start paying off the debt we have accrued.

It was pretty simple really, we have horses, and she enjoys jumping. One day she decided she wanted to buy a set of horse jumps to have for herself, a set of horse jumps that would have cost about $5,000! That was just too much money to spend on something that was a hobby, and I knew they really wouldn't hold their value, so her dream of having a set of horse jumps seemed to be short lived.

Then I decided maybe I could build her a set, and I did. And then one day I got the bright idea, with the help of my wife, maybe I could build some jumps to sell. And I did. And then she started a website for her horse jumps. Now because of this little business, we are both creating a product that people want. Because of that, we have been able to add to our skills as well as adding supplies to help us be more self-reliant. She also put together a how-to book that explains the process for someone on a budget...like me.

You don't have to make horse jumps, but think outside the box. What can you do that someone else might want?

3. eBay

Don't overlook eBay! You can make a nice little profit either selling items around your house on eBay, or even making something and selling it. If this is something you would like to look into, go to eBay and look up things that are selling.

Let's say you have a large collection of beanie babies you were thinking about selling. Go to eBay's site, and type in beanie babies, or whatever it is you are selling. You can see how competitive it is, and what items are selling for.

If you want to see what previous items have sold for, under the advanced search tab, check off completed auctions. Not only will you see what items have sold for, but you will even see items that didn't sell. It is a great tool to see if what you are selling is marketable for eBay, and hopefully, you will see if there is a potential for you to make some money.

4. Craigslist

A friend of mine has actually done really well with this, but she is a little bit more assertive than I am. First, she drives around, and finds things that people are throwing out, and she picks them up. Yes, she goes around on trash day, and gets items out of the trash. This may not be for everyone, but she doesn't seem to mind at all. And it has worked well for her. She finds her "treasures", takes them home, cleans them up, and then sells them on Craigslist, or other websites.

The last I knew, she had made about $4,000 in a little over 2 months. So not only did she save things from going to the landfill, but she made money doing it. And, more importantly she has been able to be a stay at home mom with her children because of her resourcefulness.

5. Offer Your Skills

There are many ways to take advantage of the skills you already have. If you have technical experience there are websites like Elance and Odesk that you can post a job and basically work from home.

If you are a mechanic, welder or any sort of handyman or handywoman skill you could post this on Craigslist or your local newspaper for a little extra income.

These are just a few options of ways you could add income to your monthly bottom line. It isn't necessary that you have to do this, but if you are looking for ways to make money, these might be helpful. You don't have to make extra money if you don't want too. There are many ways to save money, but sometimes having an option to making extra money can help you to achieve the goals you are aspiring to.

Reduce Your Spending

Some of these might be obvious and there are some that are not even on this list, but if we take a hard look at what we spend on a daily basis you might be surprised at how much you spend on stuff you really don't need. And you would be surprised at how often you can talk yourself into buying something you could really have done without, and I'm speaking from experience here.

Watch Your Pennies and the Dollars Take Care of Themselves

1. This might not be too popular if you have teenage children, but what they don't know won't hurt them right? I will just hang a shirt up in my daughter's closet and she will say "where did this come from?" and she loves it.
2. Downgrade your package or get rid of it completely. You can buy two movies a month for half the price of cable, and eventually have a pretty large library.
3. Have a garage sale or sell some unwanted junk on eBay, you would be surprised at what people need that you think is junk. You can also buy used clothes on eBay.
4. Focus on buying mostly sale items at the grocery store or generic brands to reduce your cost.
5. Expenses like magazine subscriptions, newspapers, or any unnecessary reoccurring bill. Ask yourself "do I want this or do I need this?" Anything that you don't "need" should go until you are out of debt or at least very close.
6. When you feel that impulse to buy that new shiny toy, make yourself wait a couple of days and see if you still feel like you "need" it.
7. The price of gas is not going down so plan your daily errands more efficiently. I could go off on gas prices, but that's for an entirely different post, the point is, there is a lot on money to be saved here.
8. This seems obvious, but any of you that have children know exactly what I am talking about. Keeping your house at a constant temperature, turning the T.V. off and turning the lights off add up over the course of a month.
9. It is far too easy to just "put it on credit" Have the mentality that "if you can't afford it, you don't need it."
10. Budgeting is sometimes easier said than done, what really helped me and my wife stay on track was the budget I created below, and it's yours free if you want to use it.

Avoid credit cards like the plague

This goes along with #9 but I just want to reiterate that it is far too easy to just "put it on credit" Have the mentality that "if you can't afford it, you don't need it." This is how people getting rich these days, by taking advantage of our "I want it now" mentality. If you have a credit card bill of $1000 at 25% interest you would pay $250 for absolutely nothing, and if all you did was pay the minimum payment each month you would be paying forever.

Budgeting – Get your personal finances in line

Think of prepping like driving through rush hour. If you're on the highway and its bumper to bumper traffic and you have 10 minutes to get to work you start to feel stressed and anxious and you grip the steering wheel tighter. The worst thing you can do in this situation is pull off to the shoulder to pass people or constantly switch lanes only to get a few feet ahead of where you were in the first place.

I can't stand these people because not only are they risking an accident that will only put them further behind schedule, they are putting me at risk. The same goes for prepping, we all have goals set and we all want to get to work on time. But if we are handcuffed by our budget and income (like most of us are) we just need to relax and understand that we can only do what we can do and come to the realization that if we try to drive between two lanes of traffic we might not get there at all.

We talked about a few ways to earn some extra money for your preps and some things you can do that cost nothing or close to nothing, so now let's talk about managing the money you already have and stretching that as far as you can.

Where is Your Money Going?

Everyone has a general idea about where their money goes, we have rent, utility's, car payments, credit cards, insurance, gas etc. but do you take into account the $5 a day you spend on coffee? Or the $10 you spend here and there on snacks and fast food? You would be shocked to see how quickly these add up over the course of a month. If we spend just $5 a day over the course of a month on unnecessary items that adds up to $150. That's $150 dollars that could be used to build your supplies, or buy that new water filter you want so bad.

I created an Excel budget planner you can find on the resources page to help you get a better idea about what you have coming in, what is going out and what is left over (if any). The reason I created this budget planner and want to offer it to you, is because it works for me and it might for you, too.

You can find the download for the free budget planner on the resources page along with the Prepping 101 intro to the prepping course that is free to everyone who has purchased this book.

I don't like putting my financial information all over the internet, and all of the other budget programs I have used were not precise enough for someone like me on a limited budget, I don't own stocks and bonds and like I said with all these company's and the NSA gathering our personal information I don't want some computer program knowing how much I owe on my credit card.

Just like any budget this worksheet is only going to help you if you take the time to update it once a week. It will take some time to plan out the entire year, but after that it takes less than an hour a week to update and change things around where you need to.

When you are making a budget you don't need to dissect everything you spend on a daily basis... that would take forever. What I do is add up all my bills and find out what I am paying out that month and then subtract the money coming in and hope there is a little extra.

Then we sit down as a family and decide how much we really need for the extras, and by really need I mean that you don't want to think too optimistic because your setting yourself up to fail but you don't want to overdo it either. Pick a good number you are comfortable with and stick to it.

So like the saying goes "watch your pennies and the dollars take care of themselves." If you pay attention to everything that is going out and ask yourself:

"Do I really need this right now? Or do I just want it?" You will be surprised how just saving a few dollars a day can add up over time.

A sometimes overlooked aspect of prepping and being self-reliant as you plan for future events is your spending and your budget. As preppers, getting out of debt is just as important as having the right bug out bag and planning for a natural disaster and even more important when it comes to the possibility of an economic collapse.

If you are struggling to pay your bills because you are constantly paying down your credit card bills two things happen...

- You will never get away from this imaginary money system
- You will be limited when it comes to spending money on your preps and working on being more self-reliant.

Start Small And Build Up.

Ok, so I started this book by saying that most books just want to scare you into buying their product and then I proceeded to go into all the bad scenarios that bring us all to the preparedness community. This is where most books stop and leave you left on your own, but we are just getting started.

The reality is, these are things that you already know, or will soon read about over and over on the internet. These are really just the basics of being educated about the world around us, and being prepared for anything that could possibly happen in the future.

As I mentioned earlier we need to take baby steps, we need to look at the smaller picture and work our way up the scale, preparing for a large scale disaster. At the end of this book there is a food storage calculator on the resources page that will give you an idea about where to start.

How to Eat an Elephant

A disaster doesn't care what race or religion you are, Mother Nature doesn't care how many children we have or how much you donate to charity, to our government we are just one of the millions of ants that it takes to build the infrastructure of a thriving society. And if a few ants have to die for the good of the colony then so be it, that's how it goes.

Because there is no one that cares more about the safety and survival of you and your family than you, your welfare is in your own hands. At its core it's pretty simple; if you fear losing everything because of a hurricane, move away from the ocean, if you fear losing everything in an earthquake move away from that fault line you built your house on. Unfortunately it's not always that simple; no matter where you live there are bound to be problems that you will have to prepare yourself for.

This book will cover everything you need to know from taking a personal audit of your situation (financial and geographic) to learning how to become prepared for a long term or short term disaster situation. Whether you are preparing for something as simple as a power outage or preparing for a complete off the grid event these prepping skills you will learn will help make you more self-sufficient, more aware of your surroundings and more prepared to handle any life changing situation.

So, How Do You Eat An Elephant?

You eat an elephant one bite at a time. Don't worry you won't actually need to eat an elephant! The point is, that even the biggest problems all start at the beginning, and as we take steps in the right direction and look back, we see that we have made more progress than we thought we did. Keep in mind that as we climb this mountain trying to become more prepared and self-sufficient, we don't need run half way up the mountain, because if we do, we will be too exhausted (broke) to make it the rest of the way up.

Prepping is a journey that will never be over, and prepping should be a lifestyle, not just a fad that we are going through. The typical view of a prepper is someone that has a house full of canned food and is so paranoid of the world around them that they own 50 guns and will shoot the mail man if he knocks on the door at the wrong time. This is just not the case; preppers are no different than any other person out there. Anyone who has car insurance is prepping for a car accident, but that doesn't mean they want to get into one. Anyone who stocks up at the grocery store because a storm is coming and they might not be able to leave their home is a prepper, we just choose to see a bigger picture, we choose not to be taken off guard by a flood, earthquake or an off the grid event, we choose to be our own insurance plan.

So just remember that if you are just getting started prepping take a deep breath, roll up your sleeves and get started building a foundation that will help you become more self-sufficient and better prepared no matter what life throws at you. Don't go out and buy $1,000 worth of bug out supplies because you are scared of an economic collapse, start at the beginning and start eating the elephant.

What's Your Plan of Action?

The first thing you need to do when you begin preparing is have a plan. A solid plan will not only save you money, it will also be a time saver. If you focus on the scenario that is most likely to affect you, or the scenario that concerns you the most you will find that you are preparing for the bigger events.

Prioritizing the events that concern you the most will help you find a starting point. If you are more concerned about an economic collapse you should probably start with everything that has to do with money, this includes purchasing what you need, lowering your debt and not having all of your money sitting in the bank. As you do this you will find that you are becoming more prepared for other possible events.

Having a plan for preparing for a disaster is one thing, but you also need a plan that your whole family knows and will follow. A well thought-out plan is only as good as its implementation, if your family is spread out in different locations everyone needs to know what their next move should be if something bad happens. This could be anything from a natural disaster to a complete off the grid event.

What about if your family is all in one place, does everyone know what to do in the event of a flood, tornado or earthquake? In events like these you time will be of the essence, if you need to run around the house collecting everyone and searching for your bug out supplies you severely decrease your chances of survival and increase the chances that you forget something that you need.

Having a plan is just like a fire drill, it might seem a little redundant but it could very well be a life saver in the event of a natural disaster or anything else your family could face. At times and depending on your circumstances it might be difficult to get your loved one and family members on the same page as you when it comes to prepping, especially when it comes to children.

Chapter 7 – Building the Community

"Be courteous to all, but intimate with few, and let those few be well tried before you give them your confidence."

George Washington

Building or having a community in a post disaster scenario will be critical to your survival. But this can be a double edged sword, we need a community to survive but we don't want everyone to know what we are doing and how much we have. So how do we do this without putting ourselves at risk?

Finding the right people that will improve your situation and not put you further at risk is a tricky proposition because just like everything else that goes into prepping, it all depends on your needs. Do you want to meet people to learn new skills? Or are you looking to form a community? Regardless of what your intentions are you need to put quite a bit of thought into it before you lay all your cards on the table.

This is the tricky part, at some point we are going to have to take that leap and make ourselves a little vulnerable. But there are ways to do this without giving away the farm so to speak. Before we get into the different reasons someone would want to create a group let's talk a little bit about what options are available to you.

Finding Likeminded People

There are actually quite a few options available when it comes to creating a prepping community. There are Facebook groups like our Apoco-List group, there are prepping and survival forums, and getting to know your neighbors through casual conversation could lead to unexpected bonds and relationships with your neighbors.

Todd @ Prepper Website Wrote an article titled "Building a Preparedness Community" that went into how to talk to someone about prepping or more importantly, how not to talk to someone about prepping. As he stated in the article...

"I think the best is to build relationships with people one on one. Find someone with like interests...maybe at church or in another group and start dropping those hints and statements that won't give you away like:

What do you think about the economy?

What did you do to prepare for the last hurricane/tornado/ice storm that came through?

Do you know anything about gardening? Etc...

Getting to know your neighbors now with simple small talk could give you an idea about who they are and what they are about. Even if you have no plans on disclosing any information about what you are doing now, it might help in a SHTF scenario to have built a relationship with them and they will be more likely to be with you instead of against you."

I posed this question to members of the Facebook group...

"Would you store extra and get to know your neighbors now without disclosing your level of preparedness to them in hopes that you could give them a reason to band together? Or do you feel that is dangerous too? I'm on the fence with this because charity in a SHTF scenario will be taken advantage of."

Here are a few of their responses...

Mary: Yes, Dale that is exactly what I'm doing. No one knows about my prepping but in case I have to band with someone for maybe their "muscle/weapons" I am storing extra. That was always part of my thinking when adding to my stash. I have only 1 person in mind. (Other than my son, who I worry that he'd be able to get here in time) it's my neighbor across the street. However, the situation would have to be really bad before I'd approach him. (He is very crafty and good with mechanics.)

Ian: Dale, But what do they bring to the party? And why should you? I guess it depends upon your situation, I wouldn't with my neighbors because I know the type they are - I think I need to move house!!!

Carla: I have decided to try to reach out to my neighbors a bit more. I don't mean telling them things that will make them think I am crazy, but just getting to know them better so I know where they might fit into my world if SHTF.

Heather: Where I am now, I only know one set of neighbors because they go to my church, the rest I pretend don't exist, because it is literally the worst neighborhood in town, but all I can afford right now. tI am considering moving to another town, not as big. If I were in a rural area with fewer neighbors I would try to get to know them in hopes of banding together if SHTF.

In my opinion I wouldn't disclose anything to anyone unless I was sure they were on my side. It might take a while to find out if someone's ideals align with yours, but if they do I think it's a calculated risk you have to take. But I would wait until I truly know them, because let's face it, people lie and embellish the facts to make themselves look better than they really are.

Forums and prepper groups can also be a great way of finding people with the same prepper mindset. You might not be able to actually form a physical prepping community but you can get some ideas and advice from others doing the same thing as you.

I say you "might not" be able to form a physical group because you never know who you will meet. You very well could meet someone in your area with the same ideals as you. But again, get to know that person or people well before you give out too much information. You should also be wary of anyone else giving out too much information to you, if someone is willing to tell you about everything they are doing in your first conversation the odds are they are lying or have no clue what they are doing.

Why Do We Need Community?

Have you ever tried to do something by yourself and wished you had one more person to help you out? Something as simple as moving a couch across the room to something as complex as building a storage shed can be done with one person, but it will take far longer and require far more energy than it would if you had an extra pair of hands. Or think about raising a barn like the Amish do, something like this cannot be done alone and requires a community.

The same holds true for prepping. There are plenty of things we can do on our own but like the saying goes "there is strength in numbers" and we have a far better chance of defending ourselves in a group of likeminded preppers.

Another reason we want to find a prepping group or community could be for camaraderie. Prepping can become pretty solitary and with everyone out there calling us crazy it's nice to talk to people who think and feel the same way we do. As you interact and become more involved in these groups you realize that you are not alone, and although you might be a little crazy, who isn't?

Be Aware of the Frauds

We all know the "one upper" right? These people that have to be the best regardless of whether they are or not, these people will always have something a little better than you have. And we all know people that have to constantly tell you how wonderful they are because in reality they need to tell themselves that to get through life. I personally trust and respect people who make me dig a little bit to get information out of them. I will to decide how "great" someone is, and if they feel the need to tell me how "great" they are I tend to steer clear of them.

In an article from the Survivalist Blog titled "Beware of the fake prepper" they wrote...

"The tell-tale signs of a fake prepper is his vagueness in answering your questions on his or hers survival supplies. The details in his prepping will be off. You might think at first he or she is being different but you'll start to notice that everything they are "doing" is off or completely wrong.

They also won't be able to tell you the companies they are using for their survival supplies. Where are you keeping the food storage? How would you get to it, if the power failed? How many people does it feed? How is your defense system? These are the odd questions a "fake" prepper would ask."

So to sum it all up, we are right to be leery of letting people into our inner circle and we absolutely should be leery. It takes longer than a week to truly get to know someone and truly know whether they helping us, hindering us or just leading us on.

But eventually we will need to be part of a community because even though there are those that have successfully gone the "lone wolf" route they are far and few between. Most of us will not mentally or physically be able to do this and will need the support of a prepping community, family friends or otherwise.

As Zach in our Facebook group put it…

"No amount of preps and no amount of training will keep a large group of people from taking your stuff if someone wants it bad enough and it's buried 100 feet underground they will get it, they will just be digging for a while. All I'm saying is that I want to be able to look in the mirror and tell myself I did everything I could to keep my family and close friends safe for as long as I could"

Just like building your supplies and preparing yourself for a SHTF scenario, we need to make sure we are making progress towards our goals and not putting ourselves at risk by having the wrong supplies or not having them at all. We need to make sure we are aligned with the right people who have the same goals and ideals as we do and are not looking to piggyback off of our foresight.

Getting Your Loved One on Board

At times it can be difficult to explain to your children or family members how important prepping and being prepared is. With the world the way it is today, and all of the different potentially catastrophic scenarios we face, we know we can't afford to sit around with our fingers crossed, but how do we convey that to our loved ones? How do you explain the importance of a situation to someone so they understand it?

Have you ever gotten that condescending stare from your children when you try to explain why you have so much food and water stored? I have, and sometimes the looks you get from teenagers can drive you nuts because if feels like you are talking to a brick wall, or you get "the blank stare" which basically means they are only listening to you because they have to, and they are not listening at all.

These principals do not just apply to children and prepping, these principles can be applied in business or your personal life as well, but it is important to remember that not everyone thinks the same way we do, and we need to take that into account while speaking to them.

Basically we need to take a look at ourselves and "teach ourselves" before we can effectively teach our loved ones to become more involved in prepping and preparing for their future. We need to try and understand "why we do what we do." Why we get so frustrated when they don't see things the way we see them, something that concerns us like our governments over spending might not be a concern for them.

We Are the Authors of Our Own Frustration

As the great Capt. Jack Sparrow (Pirates of the Caribbean) said "The problem is not the problem. The problem is your attitude about the problem."

When we let external situations determine the choices we make, we get frustrated, and frustration shapes our behavior. When we get frustrated, without even knowing it we are giving our children control over us (they are really good at this by the way.)

A child's field of experience is much different than ours, children are invincible right? Well they think they are anyway. Children don't understand losing a job or what supporting a family is like because they have never had to, they don't understand that we could lose everything in an instant because everything is provided for them (like some of the entitlists today.)

Here is an example: let's say I tell my 8 year old son that he needs to put his shoes where they go and not to just leave them lying around the house. Then he proceeds to throw them across the room towards the front door, where the rest of us put our shoes. Here comes the frustration! I proceed to tell him what the rules are, how we don't throw stuff around the house, how I pay the bills and do the cleaning and maintenance. Do you think he really cares or understands why I am frustrated? Nope! Because he is 8 he has a completely different outlook on life than I do, he doesn't care about bills, and he just knows the lights work.

But because I got frustrated I lost sight of what my main goal was "put your shoes by the door." and started yelling about how lazy that was and ended up getting into a debate with an 8 year old. If I had chosen my attitude, and made a conscious decision to not "freak out" in the beginning, I probably could have explained my perspective or "spoke to his listening" a little better. However he is 8, so maybe not.

We control our outlook; we control how we choose, so until we make a conscious decision to not let frustration control our actions and approach the situation with a different mindset, we will probably keep doing the same thing over and over.

Albert Einstein's definition of insanity is exactly that: doing the same thing over and over again and expecting different results.

The moral of the story: Don't let your children drive you insane...easier said than done right?

We probably need to take a step back and ask ourselves...

- Am I speaking to their listening?

- Am I letting my frustration determine my actions?

- Have I been consistent?

As I said before you need to "speak to their listening" meaning your loved ones need to understand what it is that you are trying to explain. When you begin to understand how to effectively talk to them, the response you get could completely surprise you. By explaining the "why" and speaking their language you help them connect the dots and hopefully have that "Ah ha" moment you've been waiting for.

Habits and Associations

Not all habits are bad, habits help us get through our everyday routines, could you imagine if we had to think about everything we did before we could do it? How long would your morning routine take if you had to consciously walk yourself through it? Like brushing your teeth, what if you had to think about every step of the process? It would take forever! When it comes to everyday routines our minds basically fill in the blanks.

Take driving to work for example, have you ever noticed that you have driven for 30 minutes and you were basically on auto pilot? Have you ever been going to the store and took a left turn because you were so used to taking that same turn every day to go to work? I know I have. It's a little frightening to think about sometimes, especially when you look out your driver's side window and see Grandma Betty driving with her head buried in the steering wheel and you think "great... I'm screwed." Our brains fill in the blanks for us, we can't afford to think about every step it takes for us to brush our teeth because we would never make it to work if we did.

Here's an example that you might have seen before:

I cdnuolt blveiee taht I cluod aulaclty uesdnatnrd waht I was rdanieg. The phaonmneal pweor of the hmuan mnid. Aoccdrnig to a rscheearch at Cmabrigde Uinervtisy, it deosn't mttaer in waht oredr the ltteers in a wrod are, the olny iprmoatnt tihng is taht the frist and lsat ltteer be in the rghit pclae. The rset can be a taotl mses and you can sitll raed it wouthit a porbelm. Tihs is bcuseae the huamn mnid deos not raed ervey lteter by istlef, but the wrod as a wlohe. Amzanig huh? Yaeh and I awlyas thought slpeling was ipmorantt.

Associations develop into habits and habits streamline our everyday lives. When I think of the word survival, I associate it with supplies, off the grid, bugging out and government. But your child might associate that with something totally different like getting through another day of school, or their girlfriend breaking up with them etc. It only takes us 21 days to create a habit, but it takes months of continued repetition to break that habit.

How Does This Apply To Prepping?

Although as humans we can "read between the lines" surprisingly well, we cannot take this approach when it comes to teaching or explaining our point of view. If we try to fill in the blanks and hope for the best I can almost guarantee that you will not be pleased with the results. If we make the conscious decision to speak to their listening and explain the "why" you will have a much better shot at conveying our message clearly.

We fall into the trap of thinking our loved ones make associations like we do, think like us and have the same cares and concerns as us. As we speak to anyone, we need to put ourselves in their shoes and ask ourselves "how can I explain this in a way that they will understand?", especially to our children.

We know the importance of being prepared for any life changing event and I believe it is our job to get our loved ones on board as well, but if this is done in the wrong way we could actually push them further away rather than help them to see that the problems we are talking about are very real.

You should also take their personality into account and ask yourself why they are so apprehensive, do they really believe you are off your rocker, do they feel like nothing is going to happen in their lifetime so it doesn't really matter or are they just to afraid to accept the reality that things are not as wonderful as they appear?

Chapter 8 – Supplies and Planning

"Give me six hours to chop down a tree and I will spend the first four sharpening the axe."

Abraham Lincoln

Build Your Stockpile

Now that you have a plan in place for what events you need to prepare for and a plan to get everyone onboard in the event that something happens, you can start building your stockpile of supplies. One thing to keep in mind while you are preparing is keeping your preps even, you don't need a year's supply of food if you only have enough water for a week.

If you think in terms of weeks and months while you build your stockpile and supplies you will ensure that you have enough food and water to last a certain period of time. One thing I see all the time is people buying a year's worth of food and then moving on to the next item on the list. If you can't last a week with the water you have stored, what good is all that food you have in the basement?

Not all of us can afford to go out and spend $10,000 on supplies and have all of our preps ready to go in a week. What most of us need to do is start small and build up. Start with preparing for two weeks. Have enough food, water, first aid supplies and all the other supplies you need to get you through a couple of weeks and you will be ready to handle any small scale disaster. After you have a couple of weeks' worth of supplies you can start to build that up to a month, 6 months and so on.

I am a big fan of lists, this might be because I am so forgetful and you really can't afford to have the power go out and find out that you only have 3 batteries for a flashlight that uses 4. I have put together a free eBook, listed on the resource page, that will give you some ideas about what you should add to your list.

It is important to keep in mind that when you are setting up a plan that you not only need to think about how much food and water you will need, but you also need to consider what you are going to do when the sun goes down and how to handle some of the other things we take for granted, like going to the bathroom.

Personal hygiene is not only important because of the smell, proper personal hygiene will help safeguard against disease and sickness. Sometimes we take for granted that everything that goes into the toilet just "goes away" but what would you do if it didn't? Or what would you do if you had nothing to "clean yourself" with except an old magazine?

Food Water and Shelter

Food, water and shelter are the three most important aspects of survival, and not in that order. We have all heard the rule of threes. You can go 3 hours without shelter, three days without water and three weeks without food. At a very simple level these are good rules to go by, but they go quite a bit deeper than that, so let's dig a little deeper into all three of these.

The Water Basics

Most of us take for granted that we have access to water whenever we want, all we have to do is turn on a faucet and water comes spilling out in seemingly endless supply. It is impossible to run out of water right? Well yes and no. On a global scale there is just as much water as there has ever been. So the short answer is no, we are not running out of water in the literal sense.

About 3 billion cubic feet of water falls on the land surfaces of the planet per year, to put this into perspective that would cover all of the land masses on this planet with about 3 inches of water, this might not seem like a lot, but consider that the above sea level surface area of earth is about 57,500,000 square miles.

Now take that 3 billion cubic feet number and cut that in half because of evaporation and water taken up by trees, grass and other plant life. About 50 million cubic feet of the remaining 1.5 billion cubic feet of water flows out to the oceans and makes it undrinkable. So this leaves 1 billion cubic feet of drinkable water that falls on the surface area of earth each year.

Around 10% of that water is used to grow our crops, personal use, for industrial use and to generate electricity. The good news is that all of that water eventually evaporates and continues the never ending fresh water cycle.

So why is that bad?

Water isn't evenly distributed throughout the planet; geographic location and topography dictate where water is more likely to evaporate and where it will fall. Another factor is population, not all regions require the same amount of water.

Even though earth is 70% water people still don't have enough clean water to drink, of the 300 million trillion gallons of water on earth, only 3 percent of that is fresh water, and of that 3% a little over 2% is taken up in iceberg's and glaciers... basically it's frozen.

This means that all of the rivers, streams, lakes, aquifers and groundwater expected to sustain the 7 billion people on Earth make up less than one percent of the total water on the planet.

These days water scarcity is a result of short and long term droughts and human activity. The average person uses 100 gallons a day and that only makes the problem much worse, much quicker.

It is difficult to estimate an exact amount of water needed for an individual, but I'm pretty sure that 100 gallons a day might be overdoing it. There is no question that adequate hydration is important, as water is a critical nutrient for survival, and your individual needs will vary based on age, gender, weight, health, and physical activity levels along with numerous environmental factors such as temperature and humidity. But this is an example of how complaisant and ignorant to the problem we all are.

Access to clean water is fundamental to survival and critical for reducing the prevalence of many water-related diseases. Civilizations have been built and crumbled because of water supply; a small community can be turned into a thriving city because of running water and vice versa.

Unfortunately I don't see a solution to this problem other than government regulation and more privatization of water, and we all know how that is going to work out. People don't worry about a problem until it is staring them in the face, and as long as water is freely flowing out of their faucets at a cost of almost nothing they will not concern themselves with how much water they use. I'm not even sure most people know that you can only survive for 3 to 5 days without water.

This is why storing water, knowing how to collect it and filter it are so important. If water becomes undrinkable we will need to know not only how to get water, but how to make that water drinkable.

Not everyone will have the option to put a 1000 gallon water tank in their back yard, and even if you do have that option you will need to protect it. It's not like you can hide a 1000 gallon tank under your bed, and once the water is gone people will do whatever it takes to survive, and if they know you have a year's worth of water stockpiled you become a target.

I'm not going to go into all of the different ways to purify water or make a water catchment, but I will go through some of the basics. There are so many valuable resources available out there that you can learn from, all you have to do is a little bit of research about what options you possibly have, given your individual circumstances.

Water Filtration and Purification

Filtering water is far different from purifying water, when you filter water it takes out the particulates and impurities, but not necessarily the biological contaminants, viruses and chemicals that purifying water would.

Drinking water that has not been properly disinfected can contain harmful bacteria, parasites and pathogens such as giardia, cryptosporidium and legionella. Water purification tablets are inexpensive, can be found almost anywhere and can be carried in your pocket or bug out bag. Other methods include boiling and using a 10 to 1 water to bleach ratio.

Boiling is the preferred method for purification but you may not have the resources if you are on the go. Water purification aside you should always have the means to start a fire regardless of the outdoor adventure you have planned.

When boiling water you need to rapid boil your water for one minute if you are at sea level, and up to three minutes if you suspect you are 500 feet or more above sea level. Water boils at a lower temperature at higher elevations because of reduced air pressure, thus the reason you must boil water longer.

Water must reach and maintain its temperature for a certain period for all waterborne contaminates to be destroyed, and the length of time it must boil depends on the temperature. For every 500 feet above sea level the boiling point of water is reduced by approximately one degree.

Some of you may wonder why not just boil water for three minutes or even longer no matter your elevation. Boiling will cause you to lose water volume through evaporation. The steam rising is precious drinking water being lost to the atmosphere. Boiling water will remove the harmful bacteria, but it won't remove the particulates. And although most particulates won't harm you after being boiled, it might not taste very good.

There are many different ways you can filter water from building your own filter in a survival situation to a store bought filter, and whenever possible filter your water before boiling or chemically treating it.

Filtering will remove debris, insects, sediment and waterborne cysts that contain bacteria and parasites. Use coffee filters, bandanas, pieces of clothing, sand, gravel and charcoal to filter your water. In some instances, not removing debris from the water can render purification tablets ineffective and the boiling process may not destroy certain waterborne cysts. The cysts can act as a shield and can withstand high temperatures and chemicals for prolonged periods thus protecting the bacteria harbored inside.

Making a water filter can be done in many different ways. You can use a two-liter plastic bottle cut off at the bottom and placing cloth or a coffee filter at the top end (cap end) and then using charcoal or coals from a campfire above the cloth or coffee filter. After that you will need to find some sand or very fine gravel and finally top the field expedient filter off with some gravel.

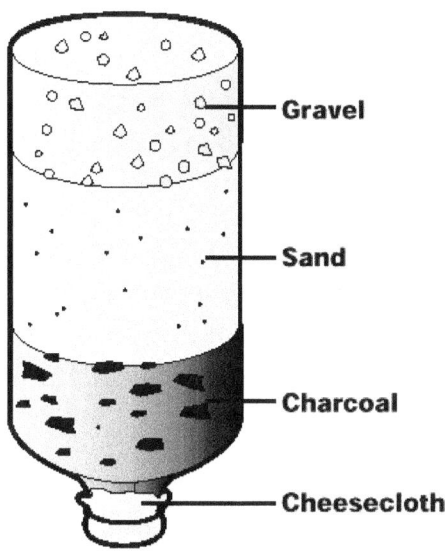

- Gravel
- Sand
- Charcoal
- Cheesecloth

But like I said, there are many different ways to make a water filter, you can use any container that has NOT been used to store chemicals or toxins as a filtering device, Milk jugs and 2liter bottles work the best because of their size but you can use any plastic container to make a water filter. If you are in a bug out situation, scavenging for a suitable container will probably be necessary and quite easy to find depending on your surroundings. And whenever possible, boil the water after you filter it.

Water Procurement and Storage

There are also other ways of procuring water when there is no "water source" like a lake or a river near you. You will have to use your imagination and think outside the box to find it sometimes but unless you're in the middle of a desert you can probably find some source of water. The concern you should have though is...will I be able to find enough water to survive? And can you make it drinkable?

In an urban situation you will be able to find water from water heaters, garden hoses, toilets...etc. if it were to rain you could figure out a way to collect the rain with a tarp funnel, dig a hole with something to keep the water from seeping into the soil, build what is called a solar still or drink the water that has collected on leaves. Like I said you will need to think outside the box.

All of these are great skills to have even if you plan on bugging in during a disaster or grid down situation. But it would be a lot easier if you already had some water stored. Storing water takes up a lot of room and considering the average person needs almost 1 gallon a day to survive you're going to need to find a place to put it all.

Water needs to be treated before you can drink it, if you are storing regular tap water it's already treated, there's no need to add any additional chemicals to it when it's just going to be sitting in a container. If your water needs treatment, do so at the point of using it, not prior to storing it.

But don't forget about what you are storing it in. Using containers that are PBA free and prohibit ultraviolet light will help decrease algae growth and maintain freshness. BPA stands for bisphenol A. BPA is an industrial chemical that has been used to make certain plastics and resins since the 1960s.

Clean your containers with a 10 to 1 ratio of water to bleach (not the other way around) for about 30 seconds and rinse them well before storage. You have a few choices when storing water, you can rotate it and make sure it is used in six months or you can add a water preserver which will help it last up to 5 years. Even if your water is older than 6 months you can still use a quality filter to make it drinkable, and it's not like water ever really goes bad, you just need to re oxygenate it after a while or it might not taste very good.

Having water, finding water and purifying water should always be on your mind, you can survive 10 times longer without food that you can without water. By educating yourself about how to build a water filter and how to procure and filter water gives you one more little advantage in a survival situation. And the more you prep the more those little advantages add up.

Food Storage

Food storage is one of the most important aspects of preparing, this is exactly why we get labeled "hoarders" or "extremists" but think about it, what is more likely to cause mass chaos and disorder, not having money or not having food? If the dollar collapse and people still have a way to eat and drink they are far less likely to "flip out" because they have not become desperate. If they have a thousand dollars and they can't buy a loaf of bread with it they become desperate and willing to do whatever they need to in order to survive.

I personally don't want to be one of these people that haven't eaten in three days and are fighting the masses for the last can of green beans at Walmart if our food supply line is cut off. This is exactly why I choose to store food as well as grow my own. Do I grow enough food to support me and my family? No, but I am learning these skills and that is what it's all about right, planning for the future.

This is why it is important to at the very least have enough food stored to last you and your family 2 weeks if not longer. A grid down event could last anywhere from 3 days to 3 three months or even longer. And it's a very real possibility that our economy could get so bad we need to have our own food source because the only grocery store around is in our cupboards or backyard.

Where to Start

As you begin formulating your food storage plan keep in mind that you don't need 50 pounds of flour and a closet full of wheat grain if you don't have the staples of your diet that your family eats every day. And if you don't know how to make bread or biscuits from scratch all of that wheat and flour are going to be worthless, because freeze dried foods you can't just add water.

A phrase that was coined a long time ago by Dr. Prepper is "store what you eat, and eat what you store" if your family is not used to eating rice every day you are probably going to have a hard time getting them to when the SHTF. Canned goods and food with a long shelf life is available everywhere and is a good starting point in your food storage plan. Boxed meals, spaghetti and freeze dried foods are also an option because the longer the shelf life, the less likely that food will go bad before you use it.

You have quite a few option when it comes to buying food with a long shelf life, you can get it from your local grocery store, one of the long term food storage suppliers like Mountain Man or Wise Foods or even learning how to can your own food. Whatever path you choose just remember "store what you eat, and eat what you store" and then work your way up from there.

Nutrition

One aspect of food storage that is sometimes overlooked is nutrition and calories. Sometimes we don't give this a second thought because there is such a variety available to us these days we are bound to get the vitamins and minerals we need to survive. But what happens when we need to depend on our food storage and all we have is Ramen noodles and rice? Without the right amount of vitamins and minerals our body's would begin to break down causing us to become sick and making a bad situation even worse.

I'm not saying we all need to become nutritionists and break down each meal based on our body's needs, we just need to make sure we have enough of these nutrients for our body's to function correctly. Our bodies basically filter out what it needs and the rest becomes waste. Just keep in mind that we want to maintain the same diet we are used to today if the S were to HTF.

The Big Picture

When you first start your food storage plan focus on your immediate future, but always keep the bigger picture in mind. You will be surprised how much you can accumulate in a short period of time, just by buying a few extra cans of something every time you go to the store you will have a several week supply built up in no time. By taking a slow, incremental approach, you will not get overwhelmed.

Starting small and building up will give you time to create a food management system that works for you. Having a food supply is one thing, but making sure it is rotated and not expired when you need it is a situation you don't want to be in. You need to store this extra food and figure out how to handle its rotation so you don't find a can of food in the back of the closet that is ten years old.

Shelter and sanitation

If you are reading this you are probably sitting at your computer, laptop, cellphone or tablet. And my guess is that you probably have a comfortable living situation, but what happens when that all changes? What would you do if the grid goes down, a disaster has destroyed your home or you were forced to leave because the golden hoard is at your front door?

Shelter is something we all need to think about and have a plan for if a situation arises that changes our current living situation. As they say you can only go 3 hours without shelter, now I know we can go all day without being at home or inside somewhere, but imagine you are on a hiking trip with just the cloths on your back and you need to spend the night, your first goal is going to be finding shelter right? A large rock that shields you from the wind, a tree to hide under when it's raining or even a sleeping bag are considered shelter. A shelter is anything that protects you from the elements.

Unfortunately we could find ourselves on an extended camping trip that we didn't plan on taking in the future and we need to have the skills and knowledge to find or build shelter. Depending on the situation shelter could be tying a tarp to a tree while you are getting to your bug out location to finding a vacant building for shelter from the elements and security from marauders to finding a place to live because a tornado destroyed your current home.

Finding shelter will be different depending on why you are without shelter in the first place, this is why it is so important to think about every possibility that would cause you to be homeless, and what you would do in that situation. Learning how to build shelter is great (and necessary) but you might also find yourself having to defend that shelter, whether that is a vacant building, a bug out location or your current home.

Home Defense

The most important part of defending your shelter is an escape plan. Unless you have the U.S. military defending your property there is always someone bigger and stronger than you, and if they want what you have, and they have the means, they will take it with or without your consent. And if our government decides that need your home for "national Security" reasons you would be fighting the military.

There are some measures you can take now to make your current home a little more secure like installing alarms, securing your perimeter, keeping all of you doors and windows locked and situational awareness.

Always know your surroundings and what poses the biggest threat. Get to know your neighbors and you will find out who the ones that are going to help you protect your home, and the ones who you need to protect your home against.

Don't do things like hide the key under the door mat, this is one of the oldest tricks in the book and could be one of the first places a criminal looks. If you absolutely have to do this use something like a hide a key that is camouflaged to fit into the surroundings?

Situational awareness is even more critical if you are in a situation where you are looking for shelter, you will need to be more aware about you environment because you will not be as comfortable about that situation as you are in your current home, and there might be someone looking to take advantage of that who knows the area better than you.

There is no way to know exactly what situations could arise that require you to find or build shelter so all we can do is learn, practice and think about all the possibility's we could face, and hopefully be ready when that situation presents itself.

Sanitation

Sanitation goes hand in hand with shelter because if we don't have a way to remove waste from our home (human or otherwise) we will be facing far bigger issues than the elements. In a SHTF scenario medication and medical help will be in short supply, so the last thing you want is to be battling a virus or bacteria caused by human waste or bad personal hygiene.

As the saying goes "don't S where you eat" and for good reason "poop" is full of harmful bacteria, A big difference between urine and poop is that urine is sterile while poop is, well, you know, not only smelly but full of bacteria, E. coli for example. So although your family might be a little reluctant I would devise a plan for "relieving yourself" somewhere other than inside your home.

There are a few options available that include composting toilets, insects that eat poop, digging a hole in the backyard to a five gallon bucket lined with a trash bag for easy removal...I'll be giving this job to the boys.

Trash removal holds the same issues as human waste, and possibly worse. If you live in an urban area you might have your trash issue figured out, but the rest of the neighborhood might not. In just a few weeks without the trash man taking your waste to the dump trash could begin to pile up causing sickness from living in an unsanitary environment, and unfortunately this will be low on most peoples list of priority's because they are starving or thirsty.

Because of the waste piling up in a SHTF scenario personal Hygiene becomes even more important than it is today. Anyone who has teenagers will understand where I'm going with this, if you don't have teenagers just imagine the dirtiest home you have walked into. When you walk into your teenagers room you find dirty clothes everywhere, dirty dishes under the bed with stuff growing on them and who knows what you would find if you looked in the closet.

Imagine this room is your home and you're going into your second month off the grid. All of these different molds, bacteria and viruses would be all over everything and even the air that you breathe. And maintaining personal hygiene by making sure you and your home are as clean as they possibly be will reduce your chances of getting sick, and we all know that sometimes when you get sick, you get diarrhea, and diarrhea can mean more than just a messy situation. It could mean dehydration and even death. It could also mean even worse sanitation issues than you were facing in the first place.

So to wrap it up Shelter is one of the most important aspects of your survival now and will become even more important in a SHTF scenario. And not only is having shelter and protecting your shelter important, you need to make sure your shelter stays inhabitable or you will be looking for a new place to hang your hat.

Start Building the House

Think of prepping like building a house, you wouldn't want to by the shingles for your roof before you even had the walls built. The same goes for prepping, you don't need to invest in personal protection if you don't have anything to protect.

Before we even begin to think about long term food and water storage or we need to think about surviving a power outage or a food shortage and work from the ground up.

In any grocery store, there is about three days' worth of food (more or less) stocked and ready to sell. What do you think would happen if something catastrophic occurred? How long do you think it would take for the stores shelves to be wiped out? The simple answer, not very long.

You don't have to go and spend $500 extra a week stockpiling food. By adding an extra $20 a week to your shopping trip in as little as 3 months you will have accumulated a nice pantry full of food. If done smart, that could be a six month food supply for your family.

Make a list of the basic things you will need in the event you could not get out for a week, a month or even three months but make sure you keep your supplies level, there is no need to have 6 month's worth of food if you only have enough water to last a week.

I created a worksheet that I used to help me stay a little more organized and focused on what I had and what I needed. Hopefully you will outgrow this workbook as I did and move on to bigger and better pastures.

Keep in mind this worksheet is for the short term basics, flour doesn't taste very good by itself and I does you no good to have 50 lbs of flour if you don't know how to use it. We also have a long term food storage calculator available for members if you have the skills to utilize items like flour, grain and rice or if you are looking at larger scale food storage.

Here's How It Works

1. On the top of the worksheet you will see "Number of Weeks Desired" enter how many weeks you are trying to stock up for in the event of a small scale disaster.

2. Enter a product that your family uses, eggs, bacon, beef etc. then to the right of the product enter how you purchase the item, for example when you buy milk it's usually in a gallon container so write GAL.

3. Again to the right you will enter how much your family uses. There are two sections "Average Usage by Adults per Week" and "Average Usage by Children per Week." Once you do this the grey boxes will auto populate for you.

IMPORTANT: You can change any of the products on the list to fit your family's needs, you don't need to add everything, just the items your family uses the most.

4. Now enter the cost per unit. The cost per unit is what you pay for the product, If you used GAL for milk you would put how much a gallon of milk is.

5. Finally, put how much you currently have on hand. After you enter this a total will pop up telling you how much you need to purchase.

6. Continue this process for all of the items you want to have ready in case of a short term disaster. Once you are done it will give you a total cost on the top right, and you can now easily make a shopping list.

You can start from one week and work your way up from there, but keep in mind that different foods have different shelf lives and if you buy 15 gallons of milk you need to have somewhere to put it, and use it before it goes bad.

Eat What You Store, Store What You Eat.

You don't want to go out and buy 100 packs of ramen noodles if your family will not eat them, and you don't want to stock up on canned asparagus because they were on sale because they are just going to sit on your shelf taking up space.

On the other hand if your family likes Ramen noodles stock up whenever you can, although they are not the healthiest thing you could buy, they have a long shelf life and can be stored pretty easily.

When you are thinking about short term, think about what you will do if you have no power for a week? Or what you will do if the trucks that deliver food and supplies to your local store can't get there? Most people don't see this as a possibility, and that is exactly why we need to have the supplies we need and stay away from the stores in situations like this.

You Don't Want To Run to The Store For T.P.

Just as important as food is supplies. You don't want to go hang out with the crazies in a grid down event because you ran out of toilet paper or you have no batteries for your flashlight. If you think Walmart is bad on black Friday, just wait until there is a food shortage, you won't just be fighting grandma for a cart.

Make a list of supplies you will need, and really think hard about this because the one small thing you forget could put a real kink in your plans. Let's say you have enough canned food for a month but you forgot the can opener (your electric one might not work) or you have 30 AAA batteries but the only flashlight you can find takes C Batteries...put your bullet proof vest on because you are going to Walmart.

Emergency Kits

The best way I have found to make sure I not only have what I need, but I know it has been rotated and is going to work when and if I need it is to set up different storage kits that contain items for different purposes.

I have one plastic container that is my lights out kit, it contains batteries, flashlights, solar nightlights, propane, candles, three different ways to light the candles and whatever else I think might come in handy in the dark....night vision goggles are next!

Another container contains personal hygiene supplies, just like the lights out kit, this can be stored in the garage or a closet out of the way. I like to keep all of these kits, containers or whatever you use in one area, this helps because you don't want to be searching around the house in the dark, or if you have teenagers and the power has been out for a week you will defiantly want that deodorant quick.

Another good reason to have your supplies organized is rotation, you don't want to have flashlights that don't work or food that is past its expiration dates. What I do is once a month bring the container in and swap out the old with the new.

When it comes to rotating food, you want to set your storage like a grocery store would as much as possible. It can become a huge chore rotating your food if you are disorganized or have cans everywhere...trust me I know. This also eliminates the possibility of thinking you are prepared only to find out that the mice have made a nest out of your toilet paper stockpile.

Chapter 9 - Lost Skills of the Past

"Tell me and I forget, teach me and I may remember, involve me and I learn."

Benjamin Franklin

The skills we have now and the skills we will need in the future could be two entirely different things. The lost skills of our past could be our future, and learning these post collapse skills now will increase our chances for survival in the future.

We might have some of these skills right now but most of the skills we have acquired over our lifetime involve what it takes to survive in modern society.

We need to have computer skills because just about everything we do now involves some kind of computer program. We need accountants, we need book keepers and we need short order cooks but how many people actually go outside and do something that was a part of everyday life 100 years ago.

None of us know what is going to happen in the next 20 years, but as they say "if I only knew then what I know now" and wouldn't it be nice to learn some of those skills now...just in case?

20 years ago I would have never guessed that I would be living in the "boonies" and married to the love of my life. 20 years ago it was beyond my realm of possibility and only a pipe dream I had occasionally. I was stuck with my "wonderful" ex-wife and a dead end job working week to week. I'll spare you all the details but I was going down the wrong path and if I didn't choose to change I was going to be stuck in that rut forever or worse.

Because I chose to change the way I did things and chose to take a realistic look at my future and change who I was, I put myself in a position to take advantage of the opportunity that presented itself 10 years ago, living with Lisa out in the boonies wearing my tin foil hat.

And no I did not write this because I know she will read it...but it doesn't hurt :)

Now I see this country going down the wrong path, I see how brittle our society is and can't help but wonder how long it will be before the economy crumbles, the food is no longer being delivered to Walmart and we are basically responsible for our own survival?

This is exactly why I want to learn these skills that will allow me to grow my own food, protect my family and heat my home without flipping a switch that the public service company supply's power to.

Whether we have decided to bug in or we are bugging out when the SHTF there are some skills that will be absolutely necessary, we can choose to learn some of these skills now, or we can wait until it becomes a reality to grow food or die to learn these skills.

What are some of these skills?

Let's say we do decide we need to bug out, and we only have the supplies we can take with us or already have stored. We are going to eventually run out of supplies and need to be self-sustaining.

Let's say that things have not totally broken down but because of hyperinflation and over usage of natural resources again we are forced to become self-sustaining. We are going to need these skills whether we like it or not.

Gardening

This is something that is a hobby for most of us today. In the future gardening could become the only way for us to feed out family. Gardening as a hobby is far different than gardening for survival, if you plant corn and the crows come and eat 90% of your crop sure, it's going to make you a little angry but today you can go down to the local grocery store and but some corn. If this were to happen and there were not a Walmart around this could have much more dire consequences.

Construction

A skill some of us are very good at and some of us have no clue how to pound a nail into a 2 X 4. I lie somewhere in the middle. I can build a dog house but it might take me a few tries.

In the future there might not be a handy man to call when your roof springs a leak, or you might not have the means to pay for those services. You might be able to patch the hole with a trash bag and some duct tape but that is only going to last so long.

Hunting, trapping and fishing

This will become a part of our daily lives just as gardening will. Getting meat to eat involves more than just hunting, trapping or owning animals. You need to skin them, clean them and preserve them because depending on where you live you will need to have some stored for the leaner months.

Food Preservation

Growing food, hunting and ranching are great ways to become more self-sufficient but you need to be able to can that food, dehydrate that food or somehow preserve that food. There are many different methods that can be used alone or in conjunction with each other but remember redundancy is key and that goes for food storage as well.

Primitive skills

Skills such as making tools, clothing, weapons, building shelter, finding water, Foraging for wild edibles, hunting and making Fire are skills that have been lost in modern society. Today we can just use some store bought charcoal and flick our bic and bam! We have a fire. How many of us can actually make a fire without using a half a container of charcoal fluid?

When the Poop Literally Hit's the Fan

Sanitation is going to become a bigger issue as time goes on in a post collapse situation. Knowing how to make things like homemade soap and detergent are not only going to be necessary to keep our home from smelling like a boys locker room but it will be an important safety measure against disease and sickness.

As time goes on in an SHTF scenario trash will build up, death and decomposition could be everywhere and not maintaining our personal hygiene could lead to sickness and even death.

First aid

This is going to be a skill that everyone will need to know and unfortunately have to use at one point or another. Knowing the basics of wound care, how to treat injury's such as broken bones and even knowing how to stitch up a wound are skills that you do not need to go to school and become an M.D. to utilize.

You will not be able to go to your local Walgreens or local pharmacy and pick up a prescription so researching herbal medicines might be your only option post collapse.

Alternative Energy

What happens when the power grid goes down? Do you have another form of alternative energy like solar power or a battery bank? Or do you know the process of making candles, making fuel or turning fuel into electricity?

Without the grid if we don't have these systems in place we are going to be forced to learn on our feet. If we are put into this situation we frankly might not survive. If the power goes out in the middle of winter and you don't have a way to heat your home you are not going to last very long.

Water Safety

Water filtration and purification could be one of the most critical skills to have. Even if water is clear and looks drinkable doesn't mean it is. There are all sorts of microorganisms like giardia and cryptosporidium that could make you very sick or cause death.

Knowing the difference between what filtering does, what purification does and chemicals you can use to make water safe to drink are an absolute necessity. Without water it doesn't matter how much food, water or fire wood we have.

The Survival Mindset

One skill that encompass all of the skills above is the survival mindset. The situation is going to be different than they are today, and people are going to make different decisions than they do today.

People will do things in the future that they never thought they were capable of, good and bad. It's up to us to decide what side of that fence we want to be on...

Do we prepare now to avoid those situations? Or do we just cross our fingers and "see how it goes."

Protection and Self Defense

Weapons and crime are going to be part of everyday life and knowing how to defend yourself, your family, your food and your property are going to be an ongoing struggle, especially in the early stages of a collapse.

Whatever your opinions about guns are now you really should at least think of them as an option because your views now could be very different than they are in the future.

What skills do you have that will be valuable if everything we know gets turned on it's head? You might be interested in this post about post collapse skills that will make you a valuable member of a SHTF community.

What do you bring to the table?

If you had to could you make your own clothes? If you had to could you bake a cake from scratch? Or if you had to could you grow your own food to feed your family? These are all lost skills from the past that could be our future. These are all skills that were required for everyday life less than 100 years ago.

We hear it all the time or we tell our kids all the time "you need to get off your butt and do something" or we constantly complain about our kids playing video games when it is 80° outside. But is playing video games really a bad thing? As they say too much of a good thing can be bad and playing video games for 15 hours straight will probably lead you down the same path as eating one whole birthday cake a day for a month straight.

I am 40 years old and I still play video games occasionally because technology these days is amazing and when I was young the only video game we had was called pong, and it was basically pouncing a dot from one side of the screen to the other. I have seen how computers and technology has evolved in the last 30 years so I understand how it is to not have a phone in your pocket at all times, but to anyone under 20 years old this is just a way of life and they wouldn't know how to function without it.

As adults we are just a guilty of this as children, there are so many things we can do these days that don't require us to leave our couch. Almost everything we do today revolves around some kind of computer program. The cars we drive, how we heat our homes, our money in the bank to how we pay for our weekly grocery's all revolve around computers and technology

The odds are that even your job has been changed in the last 30 years due to advances in technology. And while all of this technology is great and streamlines our daily lives what would we do if the electricity at your local grocery store was out or they couldn't take your debit card?

I personally believe we are evolving into becoming more intelligent and depending on our brains rather than our Brawn, could this mean we will someday evolve into those little green men we see on T.V? I don't know about that but everything we do today requires more cognitive skill than was required less than 100 years ago because everything we do is computerized or technology does the heavy lifting for us.

Sometimes as we look forward and plan our future we need to look back and remember where we came from. The same technology that affords us these luxuries today could be taken away by an EMP, our failing infrastructure or even cyber terror which is becoming a greater possibility as the days go on.

If you truly had to use them, do you know any of the lost skills listed below? What if your life or the survival of your family depended on it?

Gardening, Foraging, Farming

What will you do when the selves at Walmart are empty and all you have left in your home are some canned vegetables and spaghetti noodles? Do you have the physical endurance to complete these tasks on a daily basis?

Gardening and farming requires more than throwing a seed into some dirt and watering it. And finding food that grows in the wild that will not kill you is always a good skill to have. Learning some of the basics of gardening and foraging now could give you a little head start if this ever becomes necessary in the future.

Sewing, Quilting or Making Your Own Clothes

Again, you can't just jump on Amazon or head over to Walmart to get a new pair of jeans so could you make your own clothes if you had to?

Believe it or not I have recently been learning how to sew and it requires quite a bit more skill than most of us give it credit for. All I am trying to make is a First Aid kit, and I have a feeling that if I tried to sew a shirt it might end up with one and a half arms.

Woodworking

I personally enjoy woodworking, but by no means would I say I am a "master craftsman." By building things like a food dehydrator or a hidden shelf unit I am slowly getting better and gaining an understanding about how to work with wood and how to put all the pieces together in a way that they actually stay together.

Woodworking will be needed to make furniture, fencing, tools and all sorts of other things. With everything made out of particle board from factories these days, woodworking is truly a lost skill and a lost art.

Hunting, Trapping and Ranching

There are many vegetarians out there but I'm not one of them. We all need some sort of protein in our diet so at some point we are going to need meat. Hunting and trapping is something that we all feel like we could do. But if you have even been hunting you know that it takes more skill than just walking out to the middle of nowhere and waiting. Anyone can grab their rifle and go hunting, but the trick is coming back with something.

The work that goes into ranching is also sometimes overlooked. It takes a lot more than just owning a few cows, you need to feed them water them and care for them year round. Ranchers could be a very valuable part of a post collapse community because of the land and resources necessary to maintain livestock.

Cooking From Scratch, Canning, Dehydrating and Preserving Food:

Let's say you have some flour, sugar and you bartered with the local rancher for some eggs and milk, could you bake a cake with that? Like I said earlier if there is no Walmart and you are the family chef, what you cook is what your family eats like it or not.

Learning ways to can food, dehydrate food and preserve food are a great way of stocking up now for a SHTF scenario and also a great way of storing food post collapse when you have excess and saving it for those leaner time.

Carpentry and Construction:

We don't need to know how to build a 5000 square foot home but could you build a log cabin if you had to? This is exactly what I am going to "attempt" this summer. I have zero experience in construction but that is why I want to do it.

Carpentry and construction will be great skills to have because even though we understand that basic principles of our homes construction the skeleton that holds up the walls are hidden behind drywall and if you don't know how to build a proper foundation your family might opt to sleep outside.

Blacksmiths and Tool Making:

In a post collapse situation the factories that make pliers, screwdrivers and chisels will be out of business. Having a blacksmith in your community could not only help repair the tools you have they could also fabricate new tools.

Blacksmiths will also be valuable for making weapons and repairing weapons as well. If you go into battle with a wooden sward that the woodworker made your odds aren't very good, but if you were able to repair an old shotgun or make ammunition your odds might be a little better.

Lost Skills of The Past

Learning a few of these skills will not only help you in any survival situation when you are the only one you can depend on, they will make you a valuable member of a post collapse community that needs an assortment of skilled people to thrive. Some of these skills could also help you become physically prepared to withstand the rigors of life without Walmart and our cell phones.

We have put all of our eggs in one basket and just one EMP or cyber-attack has the potential to wipe away this spider web of technology we depend on today for months if not years. And although I do believe that technology will always be a part of our future my question is will we learn from this? Or will we rebuild the same monster with a different face?

In the event of an economic collapse or any event that causes us to be off the grid for an extended period of time, we will have to go back to our roots, I don't mean back when we were younger, I mean back to our grandfathers roots. In the worst case scenario we will need to rebuild society from the ground up. As it has always been throughout history we will need different individuals with many different skill sets to create a functioning and thriving society. So you need to ask yourself in a post collapse scenario, what do you bring to the table?

Bartering will become the new currency post collapse, and having a skill like carpentry could be a good bartering tool to have. Today we trade time for money, post collapse we will trade work for food, clothing, or anything else our family needs.

For the most part, we will not have to go back to the dark ages and live by oil lamps and ox's pulling plows, we have the technology in place to rebuild as long as we have the right people who can find a way to make this technology work. If I am able to put together a good system to harness solar power I am going to do that rather than live by candle light. We have the tools and technology we need to make our lives easier, we just need the right people to make it work.

One thing to consider about post collapse life will be lawlessness, the "entitleists" will always want to take what you have because it is easier, and will always be looking for a way to make a quick profit no matter how they have to do it. We will need to be able to protect the things we have stockpiled, and if we have created a

stable living situation and have a sustainable food source, someone will always feel "entitled" and want to take it from you. Being able to protect what you have is just as important as having it in the first place.

Here is a list of some of the valuable skills that a society will need to have in order to rebuild and grow into a lasting, thriving community. Some skills will be more sought after than others, but having some sort of skill that enables you to bring value to a community will help you out. Someone has to clean the outhouse right?

1. Farmers

For obvious reasons a community is going to need farmers, someone knowledgeable about how to maintain a food source for an entire community. Most people will probably have their own gardens but having a large food supply would be needed if your crops did not yield enough to feed your family.

2. Construction Workers

Most of us can build something that resembles a house with 4 walls and a door, but if you want to have a solid homestead you will need a good home. While over time we can learn this skill we might need to barter for a carpenter's service.

3. Doctors / Medical Experience

This could be one of the most valuable skills to have, sometimes we can diagnose a problem, but sometimes it goes beyond our skill level and we need to ask advice from someone more knowledgeable than us. There could also be some sort of outbreak and we will need someone with the skill to diagnose it.

4. Architects

Architects might not be very important in the early stages of post collapse life, but their skills will become more valuable as the community grows and expands. When it comes to protecting your preps and your family you will want to have your home as fortified as possible...just ask the architect.

5. Gunsmiths

Just like the wild wild west guns and ammo are going to be in great demand. A blacksmith will be good for not only making new guns, but fixing existing guns and reloading ammo. Ammo could even be a good bartering tool, but I don't think I would want to give someone something they could possibly kill me with, and ammo could be a precious commodity.

6. Alcohol Production / Beer

Believe it or not there are some good uses for alcohol other than drinking, such as using it as an disinfectant and/or pain reliever. Knowing how to make beer and knowing how to make alcohol would be a valuable bartering skill to have. Used in moderation Alcohol, wine and beer are great for unwinding and moral, but there are some that will exploit this on the black market.

7. Black Market

People will always have their vises, and someone will always be looking to take advantage of those vises. Anyone having alcohol or drugs will open a black market. Although anyone that is willing to trade food, water or ammo for a bottle of booze will not last long anyway. Prostitution and bootlegging will also be a big part of the black market, making these valuable "skills" as well. I hesitate to put alcohol in this category because there are some good uses for alcohol, but I think this will get exploited in a post collapse situation.

8. Self Defense / Trainers

Protecting what you have will be just as important as having it in the first place, learning how to defend yourself might make someone looking to loot you look in another direction.

9. Wildlife Experts

Anyone can grab a rifle and go out in the woods and hunt, but the trick is to actually come back with something. Having a skilled woodsman or two will help train the community about trapping, hunting, tracking and all around survival skills. A wildlife expert would also be able to barter with fur and meat from a kill.

10. Electricians

Just because the grid will be down does not mean we need to go back to the stone ages. we have technology in place and an electrician would be able to find a way to harness solar power, and fix some of the basic items like short wave radios, cars, lights etc.

11. Teachers

Again, in the beginning teachers would not have much to offer, but as the community grows you will need to create an environment that lets kids be kids and educate them to become leaders and to insure the future growth of the community.

12. Ranchers

There might not be a McDonald's around anymore, but that doesn't mean we need to go without a good steak. Ranchers and farmers are a cornerstone of a thriving society.

13. Military / Police

Some sort of police force will be necessary to maintain the peace. Crime and violence will be at its peak in the beginning, so some form of law will be needed. These people will also be needed for the bootleggers, black markets or anyone who has the means to hire them to protect their goods.

14. All Around Handy Man

A handy man might not have the expertise that the blacksmith or the architect does, but a handy man could do odd jobs for a lower price than it would take to hire a more skilled person.

15. Cobbler / Shoe Maker

A cobbler or shoe maker is not talked about a whole lot, but believe me, Nike will not be around and eventually your combat boots are going to wear out.

16. Veterinarian

A veterinarian could be a rancher's best friend. Keeping livestock, chickens and other animals healthy will be a necessity when a chicken becomes more valuable than gold...and while i'm talking about gold, don't barter your gold, it will regain its value and you could be sitting pretty in the future.

17. Politician

I hate to put this one in here, but the truth is we are going to need some sort of government for a society to grow. A public speaker would also fall into this category because of their ability to rally people together.

18. Blacksmith

The blacksmithing skill will be very valuable post collapse. Most people don't even know what type of metal a certain job requires. Blacksmiths could also fashion weapons, knives and farming tools.

19. Auto Mechanics

If a biologist could figure out a way to create a combustible fuel automobiles and farm equipment could make life much easier post collapse, but you need a mechanic to make sure these machines continue to run.

20. Biologists / Scientists

We are going to need someone who will take on the role of mad scientist, and since necessity is the mother of invention, there is no better time than the present. Scientists could help doctors, blacksmiths, gunsmiths and farmers find new ways to make life a little easier.

21. Engineers

An engineer could have any sort of background such as, electrical, mechanical and manufacturing to fabrication. An engineer could help the construction worker or the architect become more valuable.

22. Priest / Pastor

We never want to forget where we came from, and whether you are a believer or not it never hurts to have a man of God with you.

23. Dentist

If you have ever had a tooth ache you know it can be one of the most annoying things in the world. Aside from the annoyance it causes a rotting tooth can also cause sickness and even death.

24. Grunt / Serf / Peasant

Someone will need to do the dirty work, as the society grows the ones who have prepared themselves for a post collapse society (you and I) will "hopefully" do pretty well and be able to help other "not so prepared" people by giving them work, while at the same time making our lives easier. Today we go through our younger years learning a skill to support our families, so i guess we can think of our prepping as going to the "Apocalypse Community College"

So What Do You Bring To The Table?

As history has shown us, it takes all different sorts of skill sets to create a thriving society. From everyone from the leader of the community to the person digging trenches or cleaning the out houses, it take everyone working together to make a society function regardless of the skill you bring with you.

My suggestion would be that if you don't already have a few of these skills you might want to learn about some of them...unless you want to clean the toilets? I don't!

Chapter 10 - Taking Action

"In any situation, the best thing you can do is the right thing; the next best thing you can do is the wrong thing; the worst thing you can do is nothing."

Theodore Roosevelt

All of the information in this book will not help you become more prepared if you don't take some sort action. Our future is in our hands and it is up to us to insure that we are not the ones standing in line at Walmart or sleeping on a cot at the local F.E.M.A. camp when everything gets turned upside down.

It really is up to us to take our future in our own hands and know that we are as prepared as we possibly can be for anything that comes our way in the future. Thinking of modern conveniences as just that, conveniences and not necessity's is one of the first steps we can take to becoming more prepared. Learning to live without cell phones and turning the light on with the flip of a switch could become a part of everyday life for us, and having the knowledge to survive without these conveniences will make a tough time a little more bearable.

Knowing what to expect and how to react when these situations arise gives us the ability to plan in advance and be our own insurance policy. And although it might make you feel like you are off your rocker sometimes by looking at every possible disaster scenario, it is something that we must do to be as prepared for everything as we possibly can. Most people don't understand that just because we are aware of all of these possibilities doesn't mean we want them to happen...we want to be ready just in case.

Making sure we have some sort of direction and goal in mind is important because we don't want to just start buying food and supplies if we don't know why we need them, or if we need them. By using the cause and effect worksheet we can get a better idea about what we are preparing for and get a better idea of the supplies we actually need.

There are a few other worksheets for you to download in the resources chapter that will also help you stay organized.

Personal supply Checks: This list will help you stay organized by doing inventory on what you have and making sure you know the expiration dates. All you need to do is fill in where you have the items stored and check everything you have to see if you need more, or see if anything is expired.

Personal Supply List: This list is broken down by categories like food, water and shelter. This list is a great way to figure out what you need and possibly think of some things that you might have forgotten about.

Budget Planner: This budget planner will help you find some extra money for your preps. There is a video that goes into how to use this budget and it will be updated every year. You can find the link to the video in the resources chapter.

Cause and Effect: This worksheet is sort of basic, but it will give you a better idea about where you should start preparing.

Short Term and Long Term Food Storage: There are also a couple of food storage calculators that will help you figure out where you are and where you need to be. The short term food storage calculator is basically a shopping list and tells you what you need for a certain period of time depending on what and how much your family eats.

Remember, all prepper are not created equal. Your situation is completely different from just about everyone else's, you can get some ideas from other people doing the same thing as you, but only you know what is best for your family.

Just because someone on the internet puts out a supply list with a hundred different items on it does not mean it will work for you. Take those lists and make your own using the worksheets provided in this book. If you live in Oklahoma you might not need an earthquake kit, and if you live in California preparing for a tornado might be a waste of time and money.

Knowing where and when to start is just as important as having the supplies in the first place. Building a good foundation will save you time and a huge amount of money in the long run. You might feel like you need to get everything done today because you don't know how much time you have, but if you want to do things right you need to make sure you are thinking about preparedness as a marathon, not a sprint. Take the time in the beginning and save yourself time, money and frustration in the future.

Building community is also an important part of prepping, but be cautious of this in the beginning. This is somewhat of a double edged sward because you don't want the wrong person to find out how much you have prepared, because in the future these people could be coming to you for help.

That being said, most people will not be able to go the lone wolf route, we need community and we need a support group if and when things go downhill. It's much easier and much quicker to literally and figuratively build something if you have an extra pair of hands.

Having community is also important because we need to be able to talk to people who have the same interests as we do, and to get some ideas about the best way to take on our current projects. The preparedness community is very helpful and sometimes it's easier to ask someone who has been preparing for longer than you about how you should do something than it is to search around the internet and try to find your answer.

Building a good foundation by planning your preparedness journey form the ground up will not only help you save time and money, but it will insure you don't need to go back and fix the things you could have taken care of in the first place.

The last thing you want is to have 6 month's worth of canned food and no can opener. Or God forbid something catastrophic happens and you feel like you are ready for it only to find out that your batteries are all expired and you are using more water than you expected to use.

It's probably not going to be the big things that make or break you, we all know we need food, water and shelter to survive but having a magnesium stick to start a fire is completely different than being able to use that magnesium stick.

One thing that should be at the top of your mind while you are preparing is that everything can be taken away from you in an instant. All of the tools and supplies we have amassed can be destroyed by natural disaster, stolen or even "confiscated" by the government, which is basically the same thing as stolen in my opinion.

We should be working on our skills just as much as we are working on building our supplies. The great thing about learning is it's a lot cheaper than buying that expensive new survival knife. Learning skills like making a water filter from scratch or knowing how to build a shelter will be priceless if everything is taken away from you and you're left with nothing.

Preparedness is not a contest to see who has the most toys and supplies, preparedness is about surviving without those supplies and using what you have available to increase your odds.

Will This Happen in Our Lifetime?

We as Americans think of a SHTF situation as living without electricity, scavenging for water and having to defend ourselves day to day just to survive, but as Americans we have no idea what true poverty really is. There are countries all over the world that think of what we call a SHTF event as everyday life, so asking whether or not the S is going to hit the fan in our lifetime is somewhat subjective because it already has in other parts of the world.

When I think about the possibility of something life changing happening in the next 20 or 30 years I sometimes second guess myself and wonder if I am just over reacting. It's like the blue car effect, when you buy a blue car all of the sudden you see blue cars everywhere, so am I just worried about this because I choose to read about it all the time?

That thought is quickly crushed by the reminder that this system is ABSOLUTELY unsustainable and anyone who disagrees is not taking a realistic look at the world around them either because they have their own agenda or they are in complete denial.

This reminds me of riding a roller coaster, as you begin climbing the first big hill the anticipation builds because everything is fine as you are slowly climbing up the hill, but you know that is all about to change.

As the roller coaster goes over the hill some people close their eyes and hold their breath, some people embrace it and throw their arms in the air and some of us know what is coming and brace ourselves for the fall.

As the ride goes on there are more ups and downs but you never get as high as you were on that first hill and eventually the ride comes to a stop. I believe we are approaching the top of that very first hill and we are in for the ride of our lives

In this article titled "The utter collapse of human civilization will be 'difficult to avoid,' NASA funded study says" stated the following...

After running the numbers on a set of four equations representing human society, a team of NASA-funded mathematicians has come to the grim conclusion that the utter collapse of human civilization will be "difficult to avoid."

The exact scenario may vary, but in the coming decades humanity is essentially doomed to some variant of "Elites" consuming too much, "resulting in a famine among Commoners that eventually causes the collapse of society."

That is, unless civilization is ready for one of two "major policy changes": inequality must be "greatly reduced" or population growth must be "strictly controlled."

There are 2 things that concern me about this article. The first is "in the coming decades" and the second is "major policy changes"

The first point concerns me because the numbers don't lie and I plan on being around for at least a couple more decades. Although it doesn't take a mathematician to figure this out, it just reinforces what I (we) already know.

The second point might be a little more concerning than the first because it basically means our only hope is socialism. When we start telling people that they have too much of something we lose our freedoms and we become slaves to the system.

This country was built on the premise that through hard work you could become as successful as you wanted to be. If we put a cap on that, we are putting a cap on innovation and creativity. This gives the entitlists even less of a reason to get off their butts and the true innovators less motivation to push on.

Flashback to the 80's

When we look back a few decades we see that we are a completely different society with even larger problems.

- The world population was about 5 billion people

- New Plague Identified as AIDS

- U.S. Bombs Libya

- There were no cell phones and the internet that we know today was non existent

- New York Stock Exchange Suffers Huge Drop on "Black Monday"

While there were events in the 80's that could have exploded into something bigger, the threats we face today have potential to be much more catastrophic.

Because population and technology are growing faster than it ever has throughout history I can only imagine what everything will be like 30 years from now.

Back to the future

The world population is projected to be almost 9.5 billion people by 2050, if we don't destroy ourselves first that is. Mother Nature has a way of protecting herself, and we have a way of biting the hand that feeds.

In just over 100 years our population has boomed. The population spike started during the industrial revolution and continues to grow at that rate because fossil fuels make our everyday lives possible. Fossil fuel is a onetime endowment, and what are we going to do when the well runs dry? How will we maintain the population? The short answer is we won't.

As a population we have the tendency to ignore the problems we face unless they affect us directly. This video is a great example, how many people think about this when they buy a chicken from Walmart?

The question we should all be asking ourselves is "How much longer can we sustain this growing population?" and if we use up all the fossil fuels how will we even produce enough food for the population in the first place?

The End of Our Way of Life

This brings me to the most concerning part...socialism. When I think about this scenario I can't help but envision a scenario not unlike the movie Elisium, I'm not talking about the space station and the exoskeleton robotics, I'm talking about the rationing, depletion of natural resource and separation of the rich and poor with nothing in between.

This isn't something that is going to happen overnight either, I for one am not going to go quietly while all of my freedoms are taken for the "good of society" and I am not alone. There are going to be other events like martial law that are deemed "necessary" to get the situation under control.

Debora MacKenzie was also quotes in the article stating...

"Every civilization we know about has collapsed: the Maya, the Romans, Chinese dynasties, the Sumerians,"

"No one has simply made all the right choices and kept going, so it seems there's something intrinsic to civilization itself."

The difference is these were civilizations in small geographic regions, we are talking about a global scale these days, and as far as I know we don't have another planet to move to.

If this country continues on the path we are on with reckless spending and over consumption we are going to lose our seat at the head of the table. With Asia holding 60% of the population we might be forced to go along with whatever global policy's that are deemed necessary.

The reality is that most of us would probably not survive this because we are not going to just ride off into the sunset and let them tell us what we can or can't do. But what about the next generation? Will they have intestinal fortitude to fight for our freedoms? And will they have the education to know what they should be fighting for? I sure hope so.

The point is something HAS to change. Someone or something has to step in and say "Enough!" or this planet will just get rid of us and start over. If you believe in God like me you believe that he is not going to let complete extinction happen. But until then what will we have to live through? And if it doesn't happen in our lifetime, what will our children have to live through?

All of this is why I choose to prepare now, why I choose to take advantage of what I can before it is all taken away. No one knows what the future will bring, but I for one want to be as ready as I can possibly be.

Resources – Bonus Offers

My intention with this book is to make it more than just the average book you find on Amazon every day, my intention is go beyond what this book offers. As I stated throughout the book you can go and look at all of the resources we have at the Survivalist Prepper Academy and take everything one step further.

You can find the list of resources here:

www.survivalistprepper.net/academy/bonus

The prepping 101 course at the Academy is a free course we offer to help anyone in the beginning stages of their preparedness journey which takes everything in this book and takes it one step further with videos, audio and downloads.

Have a look at the Prepping 101 Course here:

www.survivalistprepper.net/academy/101

First 60 days FREE Membership
At the Survivalist Prepper Academy

All you need to do is forward us the receipt to dale@survivalistprepper.net and we will send you a link that will give you a 60 day membership absolutely free! The Academy has courses on preparedness and living off the grid. We are constantly adding courses to the academy along with free downloads, contests and webinars.

Academy members also get all of the other books Lisa and I have written or write in the future.

www.ingramcontent.com/pod-product-compliance
Lightning Source LLC
Chambersburg PA
CBHW070421290526
45791CB00005B/1789